Threads of Evidence

The true story of
our family
clothing business
rocked by one
of the most
bizarre crimes
in retail history

Remembering...

This story begins, for the most part,
some forty years ago and ends in the
present day. Because time has a way of
stealing the sharp edge of one's
memory, the details and timing are
accurate to the best of my recollection.
The essence of my story remains true to
what happened. To those who were part
of my story, thanks for the memories.
To you who have bought my book,
thank you and enjoy!
—*Jim Jensen*

Published by Jensen Business, Inc.
1212 Southridge Rd
New Ulm, MN 56073
507-354-5855

Threads of Evidence
by Jim Jensen
First Edition

ISBN # 978-1-4507-6086-7

Printed in the United States of America
by Corporate Graphics, North Mankato, Minnesota

Dedication

For my wife and best friend,
Konnie, who picks me up when
I fall, and fills me with
inspiration to attempt the
impossible.

Thanks Much,
Enjoy!

Jim

Acknowledgements

Thanks to:

• Bruce Fenske for assisting in my research of the news articles in *The Journal*.

• Steve Muscatello for photographing copies of *The Journal* news articles.

• The staff at the Brown County Courthouse for their help and courtesy during my research of the documents and transcripts of the hearings.

• Bob Burgess, Darla and Allan Gebhard and the staff at the Brown County Historical Society for their great service and help in my research.

• My former employees and all the people who are part of this story.

• Steve and Gay Jacobson and Jim Brand for their help and recollections.

• Eldon Traulich for his courage, honesty and friendship.

• My editor Connie Anderson of Words and Deeds.

• My book designer and formatter, Mitch and Eileen Madsen of Madsen Ink

Sources:
Photographs and news articles . . . . *The Journal, Billing Gazette*
Transcripts and documents. . . . . Brown County Courthouse
Research files . . . . Brown County Historical Society
Police investigation reports . . . . New Ulm Police Department
Quotes. . . . . Harvey Mackay, reprinted with permission from
        nationally syndicated columnists Harvey Mackay, author of the New York
        Times #1 bestseller *"Swim with the Sharks Without Being Eaten Alive."*
    Gordon Dean, Sir Winston Churchill, Vince Lombardi, Will Rogers, Zig Ziglar
Walt Woodard photograph . . . . *Rodeo* Magazine
Crazy Days photograph . . . . *Springfield Advance Press*

Contents

Introduction

New Ulm is a beautiful city nestled in the river valley of southern Minnesota. The German immigrants chose the location because of the Minnesota River and the rich soil of the gentle rolling hills. When I was a young boy, we would drive to Kasota, Minnesota, to visit Grandfather and Grandmother Berberich who owned and operated a small combination tavern and grocery store. Grandma and Grandpa would let us sit at the lunch counter and have a treat while we watched the old-style television set on the wall. Grandpa had asthma and died young; Grandma lived a long and happy life. She had a beautiful smile and was so kind.

We would drive home after a visit, heading for our farm home near Morgan, Minnesota. As we approached New Ulm from the east side on Highway 14, my dad would ask me, "Jimmy, how would you like to live in a big city like that someday?"

Because the city is built on the river banks and up the hills of the valley, it looks much bigger (than its 13,000 population) at night with all the sparkling city lights. New Ulm is a rare beauty as you drive in from any of its main roads. The city is rich in German heritage and charm. The downtown has been well kept with stunning architecture. When you tour our town, you'll find neat and clean homes. Our residents take tremendous pride in maintaining their property. The area of Brown and Nicollet Counties boasts some of the best farm operators and finest farm ground in the Upper Midwest. We are the home of the August Schell Brewery, one of the nation's oldest and most successful family-owned breweries, still going strong and prospering. New Ulm and the surrounding communities have a blend of agriculture, retail, manufacturing, and services that provide jobs to help sustain the local economy.

Picturesque and charming New Ulm also has been through tough times, such as the Dakota Conflict of 1862, the passion and issues surrounding World War I, as well as tornados and personal hardships. Most of the citizens are very good people. But, as you shall see in this true story, the word most, unfortunately, is appropriate. The people are honest and hard working; the majority are quite religious. New Ulm is a wonderful place to live and raise a family. The people here have a special spirit. They love to have a good time by celebrating their proud heritage. New Ulm boasts great beer, delicious German food, and some of the most famous polka musicians of all time. When it comes to sports, most residents love the game of baseball, with a strong tradition and passion for supporting and mentoring baseball players from Little League to the Professionals. We have beautiful historic ball parks and great competition. My city is a very special place, and the setting of my story.

The year is 1976. Gerald Ford is president of the United States of America. Gasoline is sixty-five cents a gallon, and it is the year before the next president, Jimmy Carter, would warn Americans of the threat and consequences of the impending oil shortage. Popular movies of the day were "Rocky," "All the President's Men" and "The Last Tycoon." Hot musicians were Rod Stewart, Tom Petty and The Heartbreakers, The Eagles, and the Bee Gees. The Pittsburgh Steelers defeated the Dallas Cowboys in Super Bowl X. Interest rates were 7.5 per cent. Leisure suits were popular for men.

I was thirty-two-years old and a partner and manager of Leuthold Jensen Clothiers in New Ulm. My wife and I had four small children. I loved my family, and had a tremendous passion for the world of business, especially retail.

My story may seem too bizarre and crazy to be true, but it is. I tell this story now because time has passed and some of the hurt and embarrassment of the past have faded. I also tell it because of all the inaccuracies previously told about the event. My intention: To set the record straight.

Most of all, I'm telling my story to give hope and inspiration to all who face adversities and hardships in their personal and business lives. My story tells about what it takes to overcome an attack on your business and family in a small town, and how the unleashing of my inner strength worked to help me regain my confidence to fight, survive, and prosper. With persistence, hard work, the support of my family, friends, customers, and a group of talented employees, I was able to continue on in business for many years with great success. Through all of this, my will to succeed became stronger as I discovered what it takes to be a winner and beat the odds.

As I look back on my business career, I share some of my thoughts, ideas and experiences which I hope will help you find success and happiness in your life and career. I will also introduce to you some amazing folks I've met along life's way. All of them are special in many ways.

Come with me now as we walk through this story of my life, and I tell you about what became one of the most talked about and peculiar crimes in the country—and how that crime almost destroyed my business. Our journey together as reader and author will wind its way through the years of an unbelievable story, and ends in the present. The part of my story that tells of the crime includes exerpts from newspaper articles, photographs and selected portions of the transcripts from the court hearings.

Along the way, I share some highlights of my career, some pitfalls to avoid and a few humorus moments that convey what I feel helped me to succeed as an entrepreneur. I've also sprinkled in some of my favorite quotes that cover my office walls, keeping me inspired, focused and excited to accept new challenges and reach my goals.

"We are judged by what we finish, not by what we start."

— Harvey Mackay

Chapter 1
The Audit

About noon, Leuthold Company President, Ron O'Brien, tapped on my office door to get my attention. As I looked up from my cluttered desk, I could see a look of concern. "Jim, let's get some lunch."

This was the time of the year when we did the annual audit to see how our final numbers would look. Our men's clothing business had been doing very well ever since I had purchased half interest from Hugo Neubauer to become a partner in the Leuthold Company in 1970. I was twenty-five-years old when I became an owner and manager. Our store was doing all the right things. We had given the store a new image and worked hard to stay ahead of the fashion trends; if an item was hot, we carried it. I was very selective in hiring the best talent I could find. They had to possess excellent people skills, be honest, fun, and really good at selling. As a result, we assembled a super-talented team.

New Ulm was a good retail community, and the men's fashion industry was strong. In 1973, we expanded into the neighboring building, cutting an opening through the main floor brick wall. After a lot of brick dust, sawing, and hammering, we took over the space recently vacated by the Fab N Trim fabric store. Now we were twice the size, expanding adjacent to our competitor, Fred Meine, Jr., (pronounced My-nee) who owned and operated The Meine Clothing Company. Our troubles began about a year later.

I didn't know why Ron wanted to talk, but I'd had an uneasy feeling lately about that year's business. Things had begun to change for our store the last year and a half. Our momentum was slowing down; we were struggling to keep our invoices current, and I suspected our inventory would be less than it should be for the second year in a row. Little signs of trouble and hard-to-explain events that kept happening gave me concern, but I would dismiss it as over-worrying and paranoia. I silently reminded myself to keep hustling, work extra hard, and "sell my way out" of my problems. After all, for most retailers, if the cash register is ringing, life is good.

The sun shone bright, but the wind felt bitter as we stepped outside on this freezing cold day in southern Minnesota to make

VEIGEL'S KAISERHOFF, MINNESOTA ST., NEW ULM, MINNESOTA

our way to the Kaiserhoff restaurant for lunch. It was about a two and a half block walk to the "K" as it's known in New Ulm. The wind whipped at my wool topcoat and made my face numb and red. We picked up the pace and hustled in a running walk, slipping and sliding up to the door of the Kaiserhoff. The warm air and inviting smell of the ribs and sauerkraut greeted us as we stepped inside. Ron loved it there, and it was our routine to discuss business over a Ray's salad (named after one of the restaurant's former employees) and a small order of their famous pork ribs. Don Veigel, the restaurant owner and a Walter Matthau look-alike, greeted us with the usual, "Do you have a reservation?"

I smiled and poked him in the side. "Sure, Don, I always do." He nodded and smiled, knowing I hadn't, escorting us to the back wooden booth area, asking the waitress to take care of us. The Kaiserhoff was the place where almost all business people met for lunch and meetings.

The waitress poured some coffee, took our order, and made the usual small talk about the weather. "Cold enough for you guys? Well, it's supposed to get above zero by Wednesday." I guess in Minnesota there's always hope of better weather just around the corner.

Her lead pencil safely behind her ear, she moved on to the next table while Ron and my conversation quickly changed to business. He was a sharp dresser and looked the part of a clothing executive; always dressed in a suit and tie. With a look of great concern, Ron turned to me and said, "Jim, what's happening with the store? There are serious problems with the year-end statement; it looks like your profit is down again from last year. The problem appears to be a considerable shrinkage in the inventory, what is going on? Do you have any idea?"

This felt like getting a bad report card from your teacher. I was defensive, "I'm just not sure, but I know our sales are up and I've been keeping the expenses in line." I knew intuitively, something bad was happening to our business in spite of the fact that things had been on a roll since I took over as manager and partner in 1970. I just had no idea how bad it was—or what was happening.

Ron asked me, "Are you sure your inventory total is right?" I nodded yes, I was positive it was right. My team was always careful to check and recheck everything. Ron suggested, "I think you should redo the inventory, and I'll come back and rerun the numbers."

Anyone who has ever done a physical inventory (counting every item by hand) knows it is a tiring and tedious process. "You really want me to retake the inventory, Ron?"

"Yes, I think we have to." We spent the rest of the lunch hour talking business, trying to remain positive, hoping things would begin to turn around soon.

Ron was by nature a very nice person and kind to everyone; he made it clear to me that he trusted me and had no concerns that neither I nor any of my employees had anything to do with the "seemingly" missing inventory. I had established a good working relationship and trust with Ron.

The Leuthold Company was a one-hundred-year-old clothing company, founded by the Leuthold brothers in Kasson, Minnesota. Their business model was to bring young people (at that time mostly men) into the partnership by selling them a portion of the business and then adding their name to the store (Leuthold & Jensen) in their town, and giving them the authority to manage their store as they determined the needs of their community. It was a golden opportunity for me and many other young people to have a chance at business ownership—an entrepreneurial innovation of the 1970s. At that time, many of the Leuthold stores had women's clothing in addition to men's. The New Ulm store chose not to include women's fashions due to the number of really good women's clothing stores already in business.

After lunch, Ron left to return to company headquarters in Albert Lea, Minnesota. When I returned to the store, I had a visit with my assistant manager, Steve Jacobson. "Hey, Steve, how do you feel about another inventory?"

His blank stare provided his answer. "Not really, Jens (the name he always called me), I'm about inventoried out. What gives?"

"O'Brien says our inventory is off. I guess we start all over tomorrow."

Steve and I had a tremendous relationship. I had convinced my former boss, Hugo Neubauer, to hire him. He was working down the street at Roiger's Shoe Store, and always impressed me with his sales ability and great people skills. Mr. Neubauer agreed to hire Steve, who turned out to be an outstanding employee, as I knew he would.

I knew he would help with the re-take of the inventory, working hard to get it done just like any other assigned task. He was never afraid of work. In the early days, Steve put his carpentry skills to good use as he and I went down to the store at night and made some changes and upgrades to modernize the store décor. Even though I was the boss, when it came to carpentry, I was the grunt, and Steve had the expertise. Together we did a good job at little cost.

Our efforts paid off; our store looked great.

> "Effort is what makes the impossible possible, the possible likely, and the likely definite."
>
> — *Harvey Mackay*

Chapter 2
The Businessman

Growing up on a farm in southern Minnesota near the town of Morgan, I think I got my interest in nice clothing from my father. Jim, Sr. was a natty dresser. When Sunday came, we (my mom, dad and three sisters) put on our best clothes and drove the Buick Road Master to the Fredsminde (Danish) Lutheran Church, just a few miles south past my Aunt Bessie and Uncle Matt's farm. I remember standing in front of the mirror getting ready for church, trying to master the Windsor knot in my tie.

My dad was a great man whom I loved and respected. He was an excellent communicator, always very honest and fair. These traits were the foundation of my future business career.

My mother, Avenell, gave me the spirit and drive to succeed. She was the most positive and motivated person I've ever known. She constantly showered our family with love and care and encouragement.

My three sisters are Mary, Marcia and Mona. I was the youngest, and only boy, so I was named after my father and grandfather.

Fits Crazy Day

MRS. ELLSWORTH JOHNSON, left, and Mrs. Jake [illegible] shown watching Carl Kingery help Jim Jensen as he attempts to try on a pair of boys' [illegible] Crazy Day. They decided he needed a [illegible] larger.

Crazy Days fun at my first job in Springfield, MN

After graduation from Morgan High School and a short college stint at Mankato State College, I set out to seek my niche in the world. My first job was at a small department store in Springfield, Minnesota, learning the retail trade from a wonderful couple, Carl and Jeanette Kingery. I loved working at the store and discovered how much I enjoyed the business of retailing.

I became immersed in the store and put everything I had into making Kingery's a great store for our customers. Carl and I worked side by side; I admired him and hung on his every word. I believe he was one of the finest men I've ever known. My training there helped shape my future business career.

Back in the '60s, the draft was still in effect, calling people to serve their country. I assumed I would be drafted and had several buddies that were talking about enlisting in the National Guard. It sounded like a great idea. I would be gone for six months of training and come back home to resume my clothing career while serving in the Guard.

I had been living the good life; eating Mom's great cooking and playing in a rock-and-roll band on weekends with my best friend and classmate, Mike Ward and his brothers, Jeff and Brad. Mike was a gifted athlete who had a deadly jump shot in basketball. Mike scored 48 points during one of our basketball games, setting many school scoring records that still stand today at Morgan High. He was awarded numerous athletic honors throughout his high school career. He was a great bowler as well, and won second place in a national bowling tournament, winning enough money to purchase a white Oldsmobile convertible. On weekends, this became our band vehicle. We enjoyed playing the great music of the '50s and '60s. During the week I continued to learn the retail business at the Kingery Department store in Springfield.

Not in very good condition, I still passed the physical and joined the Army. After being processed through their system, I was headed to Fort Polk in Leesville, Louisiana. Carl Kingery promised to rehire me when I completed my training and was back at home.

I was somewhat unprepared for what I was about to encounter. I left home, boarding a train in Albert Lea, Minnesota and headed south for Fort Polk. I hadn't been on a train since second grade when our District 49 country school class took a train ride to New Ulm.

The shrill train whistle pierced the quiet morning air as the train shuttered forward. The steel rails clacked in a steady rhythm as we began our journey heading through one new state and then another; I was fascinated by what I began to see. The world became so much larger than I'd ever imagined. I was really enjoying my train ride into the southern states. I settled into a comfy seat, stretched out my legs and gazed out the window. I saw the small homesteads where black people were working with mules, and others sitting on porches, rocking and relaxing. I found it very fascinating and honestly, I had really never seen many black people in my life. I was brought up to respect all people and had no prejudice. Part of what I was looking forward to would be meeting the soldiers who came from all over the United States. While I was stationed at Ft. Polk, one thing I did see was the prejudice some people had for black people, and it appalled me. Our country has come a long way in our attitude about how we judge people who are different in one way or another. I hope I live to see a world where we respect,

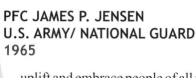

PFC JAMES P. JENSEN
U.S. ARMY/ NATIONAL GUARD
1965

uplift and embrace people of all races and cultures. When we arrived in Leesville, Louisiana, we were loaded on trucks and were transported to our barracks to be issued our clothing and equipment. My first encounter with the reality of basic training came when Sergeant Bayona started screaming in my face that the Army doesn't tolerate people that aren't in good physical condition. His spit splattered all over my face as he yelled at me toe to toe and nose to nose. I had just been welcomed to my new job and baptized by the United States Army! He would make good on his threat. I was about to find out what it's like to hit the ground running. My basic training was hell for me and the handful of other recruits that were somewhat overweight. We were subjected to extra workouts, extra job detail, no passes on weekends, and a restricted diet. The hot Louisiana sun and humidity, combined with a full back pack and rifle, made it almost unbearable when jogging to the rifle range. I would feel the sweat running down my back, pooling at my feet.

I was being transformed from an out-of-shape clothing salesman into a lean, mean, fighting machine. The pine trees, pigmy rattle snakes, and unrelenting heat and humidity would greet us every morning as we were up and running at 4:00 a.m. At first, I despised and hated the Army and what they were doing to me, but then, after a while, I begin to feel good about getting into better physical condition and decided to dedicate myself to making the most out of my experience at Fort Polk.

After six months of intense training, I returned home sixty pounds lighter, with short hair. I felt incredible. My mom and dad didn't recognize me, walking by me in the airport in Minneapolis..

My experience in basic training was very positive. I learned respect for what the military is all about, and how fortunate our country is to have dedicated people who serve our country, especially those soldiers who serve our country during the time of war. They put their lives on the line every hour and every day so that we can enjoy freedom and peace at home. Yes, I was glad to be home!

Back home, I was living the good life again on the farm, and loving my job in Springfield. However, I wondered what else was out there for me. I told Carl and Jeanette that I was giving some thought to moving to Minneapolis, and seeking a job at a larger men's apparel store. They were supportive of what I wanted to do, so I started talking to various clothing company salesmen about what might be out there for a good job.

After work one Friday night, I stopped to visit some friends at a house party in Morgan and saw the woman I would fall in love with and marry. I was instantly smitten by a very pretty girl with gorgeous brown eyes and a beautiful smile. Konnie and I have been blessed with four children and nine grandchildren. We've had a wonderful 45-year marriage, and have been a great business team through the good times and bad times. She has always been my solid rock when I was in need of a confidante or someone to whom I could vent my problems. She is not one to seek recognition, but has been my inspiration and the balance in my life. My children and grandchildren adore her. She is the ultimate mom and grandmother.

While Konnie and I were dating, I had several interviews in Minneapolis at some of the well-known men's clothing stores. On my way to one of those job interviews, I stopped in New Ulm to visit my sister and brother-in-law; Mary and Lyle Johnson. While I was in New Ulm, I thought I would go downtown and say hi to Red Wyczawski, the manager and part owner of Green Clothiers. I liked Red and had purchased a suit from him when I graduated from high school. At that time he was writing sports columns for The Journal and had written about my playing football and scoring an 85-yard touchdown after intercepting a tipped pass. Red's sports article headline read "Defensive lineman's dream comes true."

Red and I had a great visit, I told him I was going to the Twin Cities to interview for a job. He suggested that I go over to his competitor (Leuthold and Neubauer) because one of their full-time salesmen (Dick Wilbrecht) had just left to go to work at 3M. I did as Red suggested, and it resulted in Hugo Neubauer offering me a job. Although I really wanted to move to the Cities, this was a good offer that I saw as a good opportunity to learn more about the men's clothing business and take the next step of my career. I accepted Mr. Neubauer's offer of employment and became part of the New Ulm retail scene. I was very excited about my new job opportunity.

Konnie and I were married on February 26, 1966 in Redwood Falls, Minnesota. I took off work Friday, Saturday, Sunday and Monday. I was back at work on Tuesday, obviously, no ocean honeymoon. We moved to New Ulm and lived in a small apartment on South Franklin Street. Konnie got a job as a teller at Citizens Bank and worked there until our first child, Christopher, was born. I liked working at the store and was able to move into a management position due to the experience I had while working at the Kingery store in Springfield.

In 1969, I was offered the job of managing the new Herberger's men's store that was just being expanded and remodeled. I called and talked with my boss, Mr. Neubauer, who was spending the winter in Mesa, Arizona. He encouraged me to turn down the job, telling me he would sell me his interest in the store in the spring; he told me he wanted to retire and wanted me to have a chance to be a partner in the business. He did as he promised and in 1970, at age twenty-five, I became a partner and part owner of what would be called Leuthold & Jensen Clothiers. We were now business owners; we just knew this was the break that would help secure our financial future.

New Ulm was a city with a lot going for it, and I wanted to be a part of it. For many people, the first thing that comes to mind when they hear someone say "New Ulm" is polka music. Getting to know some of the greatest polka musicians was really fun for me because I love their music. It was a treat to meet many of the great musicians when they came into our store. They were so interesting and entertaining with so many stories to tell. Of course, I appreciated the fact that they were customers and promoted our city, encouraging folks to shop in all of the New Ulm stores. When I was a sophomore in high school, I came to New Ulm on a Saturday night for my first trip to George's Ballroom. I just couldn't wait for the dance to start at the big ballroom. The band was the famous Harold Loffelmacher and The Six Fat Dutchmen.When they struck up the band, the sound from all the brass horns thumped against my chest. I was awestruck. The sound was so incredible; I'll never forget that moment as long as I live. Their band played all over the United States, and was a featured group on the Lawrence Welk show on Network Television.

Another hugely popular New Ulm band was The Whoopee John Wilfahrt Band. I listened to them on the radio on Saturday night as a young boy. We would gather around the big Montgomery Ward Airline console radio at our farm home listening to the announcer say, "Live from the Prom Ballroom, downtown St. Paul, Minnesota, it's Whoopee John Wilfahrt and his orchestra.'" The music would play and my three sisters and I would dance our hearts out on the living room floor.

George Neuwerth was the founder and owner of George's Ballroom, home to many of the great bands who filled the place on Saturday nights. I can still picture George sitting on a stool at the entrance of the ballroom with a cigar in his mouth, wearing his fedora hat as he greeted his customers. In all my years on Minnesota Street, George's was one of the most-frequently-asked-about landmarks by visitors. It was the grandest of ballrooms and most spectacular in the early days. The complex included a huge ballroom, the longest bar in Minnesota and a bowling alley. George and his wife Ella were very gracious hosts to many of the top bands of the '40s, '50s and '60s. Yes, the place to be on Saturday night was George's!

The polka beat goes on today with the great Wendinger Band, Johnny Helget, The Bock Fest Boys, Leon Olson and many others. I hope the music never dies; it is the heartbeat of New Ulm.

Our city is home to the Minnesota Music Hall of Fame located downtown. The Hall is worth taking the time to visit to relive the glory days of New

Ulm's Polka music history as well as the Minnesota legends of all venues of music.

This was our home, and we were in business. We had the world by the tail.

During the period of the late sixties through the late seventies, our town had four men's clothing stores: Green Clothiers, Spelbrinks, Meine's and Leuthold & Jensen. For the most part, we were all on friendly terms and helped each other when needed.

Red Wyczawski was a partner of Green's and was also the town mayor. He was a great competitor and is still a good friend. He has a love for sports and worked for the Milwaukee Braves baseball team prior to marrying Mary Green and moving to New Ulm to become a retailer.

Bob and Ron Spelbrink were friends as well. Fred Meine, Jr. was right next door to our store and his operation was somewhat outdated. Mr. Meine was the owner of one of New Ulm's oldest clothing stores, taking it over from his father who was a very successful businessman. Fred often wore a dress hat, black-rimmed glasses and carried a walking cane.

Konnie makes great chocolate chip cookies. When she would make a batch, she would bring some to the store for the employees and on occasion, would bring an extra sample for Fred Meine, Jr. When the Minnesota snowstorms would bury us, I would sometimes ask my employees to shovel Fred's sidewalk for him. Although he was mostly indifferent and somewhat aloof, we thought he was a decent man. However, some felt he had a mysterious and shadowy demeanor.

Meine's business appeared to be slow, while ours was on fire. When I would come in to chat or see if he was alright, he would meet me at the door and keep me in the front area of his store. I always wondered if he was embarrassed about his store and didn't want me to see his dated inventory and older style of operation. The Meine store was often dimly lit and had a unique odor that reminded me of a mixture of stale fabric, and musty leather. His store fixtures had literally become antiques. It looked like Fred was doing very little business, and I wondered how he could possibly make it. In spite of his apparent uneasiness towards me and my family, we still tried our best to be good business neighbors. As time went on, I rarely saw Fred or went into his store as I felt somewhat unwelcome. I guess we really never knew just what to think about Fred Meine, Jr., our neighbor.

"They used to say that what you see is what you get. In truth, what you think is what you get."

— Harvey Mackay

Chapter 3
Where's the Leak?

I was visiting with my secretary (and sister) Mary Johnson about an upcoming sale when the store telephone rang. Mary answered it. "It's for you; Ron O' Brien is on the line."

Ron said, "I'll be in New Ulm on Tuesday. Have you finished redoing the inventory?" I told O'Brien the work was completed.

"How's it looking?"

"About the same as before; maybe a couple hundred more. We found a few layaways and return items that hadn't been counted," I responded.

Ron repeated that he'd be over on Tuesday to re-examine the books. I went home for lunch and told Konnie, "I'm convinced someone is stealing our merchandise."

"You mean shoplifting?" she asked.

"I don't know, maybe," I replied.

My wife, who was and still is the voice of logic said, "Well, don't worry yourself sick. I know it's been on your mind a lot, but you're doing everything you can. Maybe it's an error somewhere in the accounting process, and Ron will find it when he closes the books for the year."

Growing up on the farm, our family just didn't ever think that anyone would steal from us. My father rarely locked up the big red gas barrel. One day when I suggested we should keep it locked, he replied, "What if a neighbor runs out of gas and we're not home to help them out?" That's the way we were brought up in Brookville Township, trusting. For that matter, we never locked the doors to our farm home either.

Many thoughts were going through my head as I finished my lunch and went back to my store at 14 North Minnesota Street. I was becoming very concerned about the future of my business. I also knew in order to pay my bills, I had to focus on the positive, and not dwell on the negative things that seemed to be happening. I had to become better at selling to increase sales to avoid going under water financially. I read everything I could find about sales excellence and enrolled in several courses on salesmanship and effective communication. I had a passion to be better at selling and customer service.

Tuesday morning was another cold one. It was going to be "one of those winters;" cold and blowing snow. I felt a sharp pang in my lungs as the cold icy air entered my body. Damn, why do we live in this God-forsaken place? My Chevy Caprice groaned as I twisted the ignition key. Driving toward downtown New Ulm on my way to work, I began to think about what

"The most important way to close a sale is to have people on the sales floor talking to and assisting shoppers. The longer the shopper stays in the store, the more they buy. Engaging shoppers and listening to their needs is the age-old solution to success."
—Zig Ziglar

would happen today. Maybe O'Brien would call and cancel his trip due to the weather; then I wouldn't have to face whatever we discovered.

We were very strict about preparing our store for business every morning. Part of our ritual was to sweep our sidewalk or shovel the snow, depending on the season. After putting away the snow shovel and hanging up my topcoat, my first customer of the day walked in. "Have you got any decent leather gloves, Killer?" Bill Huevelmann always called me by that; I have no idea why. Every store it seems has an ambassador of sorts. By that I mean someone who spends quite a bit of time hanging out at the business, and becoming a big booster. Bill was in the store so much some people thought he worked there. He became very close to our family and employees. My mother would visit the store and, on certain occasions, bring a fresh pie or cake and always insisted that we have Bill come down to get a slice. He loved Mom's baked treats and she loved that he enjoyed them.

Bill is retired now, but is one of New Ulm's most interesting people and a well-known tax consultant. Bill's office was upstairs just two doors to the north on Minnesota Street, making it handy to drop in for his frequent visits. At that time he was the secretary of the Brown County Fair Board. Back in those days, the Brown County Fair was one of the top county fairs in the state. Bill insisted that I become involved by serving on the fair board. I served several years and had a great experience working with the Matt Armstrong Carnival, the professional rodeo and the country music shows. I can still hear Bill's distinctive voice booming across the midway saying, "Folks, get those tickets now for the Joey Chitwood Thrill show in front of the grandstand."

Bill has a very dry and witty sense of humor, and tries to give you the impression that he is crusty and tough; in truth, Bill is one of the kindest, nicest people I've ever known. I know my involvement on the fair board was one of my best networking opportunities and was important to my business success. It pays to get involved in your community in so many ways.

> "I used to say that networking is the most underrated management skill. Now I believe it may be the most important management skill, bar none."
> — Harvey Mackay

Ron O' Brien arrived at about 10:00. "Jim, your store looks great! I like the way you've rearranged the displays and departments." I was thinking this must be the good news/bad news scenario. You know, first the good news. I thanked him and invited him to come back to my office where we could lay everything out.

After going over the entire year-end statement, it looked bleak. My inventory was short by thousands of dollars. I looked at Ron, asking, "So, where's the leak?"

Ron had given me a lot of support and had confidence in my ability to be a manager. In fact he would call me and ask me to visit and coach some of the Leuthold Company store managers who were looking for some fresh ideas. "It's either a lot of shoplifting or employee theft," he suggested.

I shook my head and said, "No, we know all of our customers. They're our family, friends and neighbors. We personally wait on every customer."

Ron looked me straight in the face and said, "Maybe an employee is stealing it?"

"No way; Steve Jacobson is like a brother, and all our employees are really like family," I insisted.

Ron was searching for a reason and replied, "Well, maybe it was a "one-time" theft that went undetected."

"You mean like someone left a door open?" I said.

"Yup, or maybe someone figured how to get in when the store is closed. Jim, let's close the books for now and keep an eye out for anything that looks suspicious. Have you talked to the New Ulm Police about your concerns?"

I looked down at the floor, shaking my head, "No, I have not." This was not the way I'd hoped the year would end. My bonus and percentage of the profits normally were paid out when we closed the books. I really was counting on that money. Our family was young, with plenty of bills to be paid. It was a whole year's work down the drain. How could this be happening? I started to get really angry about who was stealing from me. I made up my mind right then and there I'd get to the bottom of it. They would be sorry if I could catch them (whoever "they" were) but until I know for sure, I won't burn any bridges.

"He who burns bridges better be a damn good swimmer."

— *Harvey Mackay*

Chapter 4

Call the Police

Bert Schapekahm stood about six feet three and weighed over two hundred pounds. He was a well known and very popular member of New Ulm's Police Department. When Bert would walk into a room, he got everyone's attention. His smile and charming personality drew people to him. He was also an excellent police officer. There is a story about Bert that I've been assured is true. Bert was on duty when he was called to check on a group of rowdy motorcycle club members that had camped at Riverside Park in New Ulm. When Bert arrived, he got out of the squad car and walked into a much more serious situation than he'd imagined. He was immediately

Bert Schapekahm

surrounded by the entire group of very scary looking men. Bert could see they were not happy to see the law, so Bert went for his most effective weapon, his sense of humor. He looked around and said, "Okay, I've got you surrounded, now what are you going to do?" I guess they looked at each other and began to laugh out loud. It was pretty funny. Bert gave them his big smile and asked them to enjoy themselves, keep it down and not cause any trouble. They visited for a while and promised to be on their best behavior while they were in our city. Before he left their encampment, Bert had extended a hand in friendship to this group of men most people would fear; in turn they gave him their respect and kept their word to be peaceful. Years later Bert became our mayor, and did a great job. How could you not like Bert, he was a friend and customer as well.

Calling the station, I asked Bert to stop by the store when he had a minute. A day or two later Bert walked into the store, and we chatted about the local scene. I asked Bert to come into my office. "What's up, Jim?"

"Bert," I said, "I think someone is getting into my store at night and stealing my merchandise."

"Are you kidding?"

"No, and I think it might be quite a bit," I replied.

I told Bert how I had noticed things missing and that our inventory count had not been reconciling. Bert asked me how long I thought it had been going on, and I told him it may be a year or two. Bert then asked me about a robbery he remembered investigating that occurred a while ago at our store. I told him "Yes, we were robbed in 1975 when someone stole a number of leather coats and suits."

Officer Schapekahm gave me that big smile, rocked back in his chair and said, "Jim, I think there's somebody out there that just doesn't like you very much."

"You're probably right," I answered. Bert and I both felt that the previous theft most likely was not related to my current problem, and suggested that he do a walk-through "security check" to see if there was some way of entry that was not obvious. I agreed, and he said he would be back the next day.

Officer Schapekahm arrived the next morning at 9:00 sharp and asked me to show him all of the points of entry. I walked him through my entire store, including the basements. With flashlights and notepads in hand, we scoured the entire store. Bert made some suggestions on new locks and other things that we would follow up with, hoping that would make our store secure. He also told me he would have the patrolmen keep an eye on our store at night as part of their routine watch.

The buildings in downtown New Ulm are really old. Some historians have told me the buildings are well over one hundred years old. The concrete floor is soft and crumbles, causing a fine dust when we would try to clean and sweep it up. The basement in my original store was the most useable, so most of my racks, supplies and display items that were still in use were kept in that basement. The basement next to Meine's store was in poorer shape, and we rarely went down there unless we had to.

When I leased the building next to Fred Meine, Jr., he told me there was a restroom in his basement that he shared with previous tenants. He offered it to us as well. Since we had our own facilities, I suggested that we close the large heavy wood door, lock it, and he would have total use and privacy of the toilet. The facility was quite crude and desperately in need of a cleaning and up-grade. Fred seemed surprised but agreed with my request. After that, the dimly lit corner of the basement that led to the common restroom was used as a storage area, cluttered with out-of-date fixtures, glass

Various downtown New Ulm buildings circa 1975

shelving and mostly unusable old display items.

People in my store, including my employees, were beginning to wonder why we were being visited by New Ulm's finest. Members of the Police Department only stopped in our store occasionally or if they were in street clothes to shop like any other customer. Their now-frequent visits began to cause a stir in the store. I confided in Steve Jacobson, my friend and co-worker. I described in detail the loss of inventory and the mystery of where and how the clothes were disappearing. He was equally upset, and vowed to track down the crooks.

Steve is a feisty guy who will stand up for what is right. He is smart and has the determination and the tenacity of a pit bull and the sense of humor of a standup comedian. Back in those days, the older people could and did speak the German language. Steve Jacobson could speak German, and was a big help when he could discuss the pros and cons of a purchase, in one of the German dialects. Steve would also surprise a couple now and then when they would be discussing their options privately in German and Steve would chime in, also speaking in German. The customers would really get a kick out of it and most likely buy the suit from him. Steve tried to teach me to speak German, but finally gave up realizing "this old dog just could not learn that new trick."

Steve was a trustworthy person in whom I could confide. We walked through the store and pondered what was happening. I told Steve, "Maybe it's over; we were robbed and somebody got away with it. Let's do everything Bert suggested and keep our eyes and ears open. Let's get back to what we do best–selling clothes and get our store back on track." We hoped that would be the last of it. But it wasn't.

"Without the right sales skills, something terrible happens...nothing."

— *Harvey Mackay*

Chapter 5
Disappearing Merchandise

Accounting/bookkeeping is not my favorite task, but when you're a businessman, it's all about the numbers. The weekly reports and the monthly profit-and-loss statements began to loom large with every update. I would pore over every item, hoping things would improve. They didn't; in fact, they got worse.

Strange things continued to happen in my store. Just one example: I'd ordered a custom-tailored, three hundred fifty dollar Hart Schaffner & Marx suit for one of my best customers. It was hung in the back of the store for him to try on at his convenience. When he arrived to take a look at his new suit, I couldn't find it anywhere—the suit had vanished! Where was it? We searched the store, frantically trying to locate the suit while the customer patiently waited. It wasn't to be found. I was embarrassed and upset. I'm sure the customer was wondering what was going on as well. I told my customer that I would reorder the missing suit, and promised the company would rush it out. He was understanding and was willing to wait.

Soon I became suspicious of everyone and everything, staying awake, tossing and turning in agony, wondering what was happening. At the store, everything (we imagined) began to look like clues. We started to "ride herd" on everyone who came into the store. Everyone became a possible suspect. It was almost beginning to look like a situation comedy for TV. Without sleep, I was tired during the day. I told Konnie, "I'm going to sleep in the store for a couple of nights. Maybe the mysterious thief will come in when I'm there."

She wouldn't let me and pleaded with me, "Jim why don't you just relax; maybe it's over and done. You're driving yourself crazy. Besides, if someone did come in while you're there, you might get hurt or do something foolish and end up in really big trouble."

Somehow Konnie's words made sense. I needed to "back off" and focus on my store. Our young children needed their dad to be with them both physically and mentally. I had ignored them long enough.

This tough year was coming to an end. A year had passed since our last audit and I hoped this year-end report would look brighter, although I knew better. Our cash flow had slowed down; we were stretching to pay the bills, and my inventory was limited. Weary, I was close to breaking down from the stress of my business concerns.

People who know me well generally see me as an extreme optimist. I love life, people, and fun and always try to see and focus on the positive side of things. I'm a people person, and abide by the words of the late political humorist Will Rogers, "I never met a man I didn't like." I love to meet new people, learn all about them and get to be friends. I love to spoil my customers and pamper them so they enjoy their shopping experience and return again and again. I love all aspects of business. It's exciting and challenging. But, most of all I love giving my customers great customer service. I believe if you focus on the positives, good things will happen. Boy, my beliefs were being challenged with my business problems. Still, everyday was a new and exciting opportunity, and I desperately needed to make my family life and my business better and more fun. I must persevere and save my business!

"Never judge people—don't type them too quickly. But in a pinch never assume that a man is bad; first assume that he is good and that, at worst, he is in the gray area between bad and good.

—Gordon Dean

Next to my family and my business, my horses have always been a passion of mine. When I was a little boy, I begged my dad for a horse. When I was about ten years old, I finally got my own horse, a gentle, older, grey mare named Mitzi. I rode that horse day and night, rain or shine, sleet or snow. I became an avid horseman. When I got older and started working, horses became my golf and fishing enjoyed by most businessmen. For me, it has been a source of relaxation, satisfaction and a challenge to make my horses perform better. Through the years my interest in horses moved into the competitive arena of rodeo and the sport of team roping. At times this would be my getaway from the store issues. When you're riding a horse thirty miles an hour, and roping a Corriente (Mexican) steer, your mind is really focused on the challenge. The roping experience and competition also gave me additional courage and determination to accept challenges, and not be afraid to put myself in a position for success. I needed to focus on the positive to keep my business from failing. Time spent away with my horses, from day-to-day commitments, was one of the reasons I could keep moving forward, and not give up.

My roping hobby also opened the door for a spin-off business a few years later. There were roping schools where you could bring your horses along with you in order to improve your skills while riding your own horse. The best instructor was world champion Walt Woodard from California. I called Walt and learned he would be having a school in Auburn, Nebraska that April. I wanted to be a better roper, so I signed up along with my son, Chris, who was just learning to rope. We would bring younger brother, Eric, along as an observer, and the three of us would take a vacation in hopes of becoming better ropers.

Our horses loaded up, we headed for Nebraska. Along the way, we stopped and visited our friends in Canton, South Dakota, the Campbell family. Pete Campbell, our Tony Lama boot company sales rep, was a cowboy and roper. We stayed at their house and enjoyed the evening socializing and roping in their arena.

Once we arrived at Auburn, Nebraska, the roping school was really great, and our roping improved to a whole new level. It was fun meeting new people from several states who shared our interest in roping; we would see them later on competing at jackpots and rodeos. The boys and I had fun roping, eating pizza at night, and having Twinkies and chocolate milk for breakfast at the gas station. They promised not to tell their mom what I had been feeding them.

No way would I have known that how I approached the world every day would change forever after meeting and listening to Walt Woodard.

Walt Woodard

Walt is a great roper, probably one of the best ever, but I believe he is even more gifted as a speaker and motivator. At the end of each day Walt spoke to us about what it takes to "win in life;" how to prepare each and every day for success in whatever we were doing. He stressed the need to be persistent and to stay focused on the positive. His message touched me, making me want to be the best person possible. He gave me inspiration to "cowboy up" and give it all I had in roping, in business and, most importantly, in life. He is a great speaker and a wonderful friend.

Later on, Walt and I became business partners and started the Walt Woodard Rodeo Collection western shirt company, selling shirts all over the world. The shirts, popular with horsemen world-wide, were made in Fort Worth, Texas.

My Favorite Horse of All Time—Peso

Amazingly Walt came out of retirement at age 52 and made a run for another world championship, winning second place. The next year, 2007, Walt stunned the world of professional rodeo and, for the second time in his career, he was crowned World Champion Heeler in the team roping event at the highest level of rodeo competition in the world: the Wrangler National Finals Rodeo in Las Vegas, Nevada.

Walt now lives at his new ranch and training center in Texas with his wife Darlene and son Travis, who is also a world-class pro roper. I feel fortunate to have met such a great rodeo athlete and inspirational person. His speaking style and skills had a strong influence on my pursuing opportunities as a business /motivational speaker.

Just recently, Walt received another great honor and was inducted into the Rodeo Hall of Fame at a ceremony held at Oklahoma City, Oklahoma.

Sir Winston Churchill is credited as saying: "The outside of a horse is good for the inside of a man." How true for me.

Chapter 6
Bad News

Ron O'Brien was coming on Friday to do the year-end audit. Things were going from bad to worse. A day before Ron O'Brien was to arrive; I went across the street to visit with my pal, Tom Lindemann who owned The Music Store. Tom and I were good friends and we both started in business about the same time. They sold musical instruments as well as pianos, organs, television sets, and stereos. Tom was a terrific promoter and always had an event in the works or on the drawing board. We enjoyed talking business and sharing ideas. He always called me "Jimmy Jensen." Up to this point, I had kept my concerns about my inventory loss very confidential, but I had to talk to someone.

Opening the big glass door to the Music Store, I walked past the rows of shinny pianos and organs, running my hands over the smooth finished wood. I loved music, and when I would come into his store, I would reminisce of my days at Morgan playing the drums in our rock-and-roll band. It was a short-term music career, but one I would love to relive to this day.

One of Tom's most unique promotions was a big event at the Music Store that featured a milking contest between polka band leader/personality Harold Loffelmacher and me (I was the Chamber of Commerce president at the time); the contest was held inside the store, using a live Holstein cow. KNUJ Announcer Perry Galvin did a play-by-play of every pull. I remember Harold "pulled ahead" of me

Cow Milking Contest in Tom Lindemann's Music Store

> **Desperate to find out how someone might be gaining access to our store, we took more steps to try to catch the perpetrator in the act. This included changing the locks and making frequent visits to the store at night.**

and won the contest. It was great fun; leave it up to Tom to think up a great event like that.

Tom was in his office near the back of the store. I often dropped in to visit with Tom when he wasn't busy selling, so my visit wasn't unusual. He said, "Sit down Jim," gesturing to a chair near his desk. "How's New Ulm's premier clothier?"

"Well Tom, that's why I'm here. I'm not so great." I began to unravel my ball-of-string story about missing merchandise. Tom listened intently as I went into detail about the mystery. "What do you think, Tom?"

He wasn't convinced about shoplifting or employee theft either. "Are you sure someone didn't get a key, and come in at night and load up and steal a bunch of your clothes?"

"That's kind of what I'm thinking it may have been, but it seems like it's still going on because weird things are still happening and more items are missing," I said.

Tom didn't have any answers, but reassured me that he knew we were probably doing whatever we could and sooner or later it would come to a head. When I left Tom's store, I didn't have any more answers to my problems, but it was helpful to talk to another business person, and I knew Tom would be supportive.

Ron O'Brien and I both knew the situation was getting worse. We looked at the second year of losses in inventory and profits as we tried to make some sense of things. My store's image in our market area was still very positive—very much a fashion leader in menswear. At clothing markets, I'd search for new ideas, colors, styles, and vendors. This, along with a combination of a creative marketing plan and a very talented sales team, kept things positive in spite of our dilemma. Our store was established as "a place to find the newest and greatest" for men's fashions in southern Minnesota. To be successful in business, you must be: "The best, be different and be the first to do it."

I always liked the advertising and promotions part of my business and when it came to our marketing, I was inspired by a long-time businessman who was a terrific promoter. Don Dannheim owned the New Ulm Dairy where they bottled and sold milk, ice cream, and various other dairy products. His business name changed to the KUHSTAHL (cow stall) and they marketed a cash-and-carry concept with clever advertising featuring BIG DON. Don used our children in several of his newspaper ads in the New Ulm Journal. He was an effervescent and motivating person whom you just had to love. Customers came from a big geographic area to take home his fresh products. He was a master marketer. I learned a lot from Don Dannheim and respected his love for business.

"BIG DON" Dannheim of New Ulm Dairy/Kuhstahl

I was one of the first businesses to use live call-in radio commercials on several area stations, as well as WCCO in the Twin Cities. These two-to-three minute "live" commercials were effective, giving me an opportunity to sell my merchandise with my voice and personality. It was our most effective form of advertising at the time, helping build our business and expand our market area.

Desperate to find out how someone might be gaining access to our store, we took more steps to try to catch the perpetrator in the act. This included changing the locks and making frequent visits to the store at night. Several security mirrors were added—and we tried anything and everything else that we could possibly think of.

I told Ron O'Brien I was finding more clues that we were being slowly robbed —almost a "business death by strangulation." We went through every inch of our business operation, painstakingly discussing every detail. The results of this year's audit showed more inventory loss. "Jim, we can't keep going on like this and stay in business. The strange thing is that you're doing a fantastic job of managing the store and increasing the sales in spite of the distractions. Honestly, Jim, I don't know how you've done it."

Quietly I thanked him as I closed the leather-bound ledger that showed a loss in profit for another year. No profit meant no bonus for me to pay my personal bills either. I wanted to scream, "Why was God letting this happen to me?" I believed that if you were fair and honest, and worked hard, you would be rewarded. I also trusted and believed that my faith in God would help me find my way through all this. I believe it did.

Ron trusted me and had total faith in my honesty and ability to manage our store. Ron was convinced that we should continue "business as usual" with a watchful eye on everything and everybody. "Sooner or later whoever is doing this will make a mistake, and we will catch them," he assured me. O'Brien was a small, wiry man with a strong and mighty handshake that always surprised me. He slipped into his wool trench coat, picked up his brief case and said good-bye to all of us, realizing another year of disappointing financial results. I wished all of this was a bad dream, and I would wake up soon.

"There are really
no mistakes in life—
there are
only lessons."

— Harvey Mackay

Chapter 7
The Suit Hangers

Minnesota winters are long and hard. Spring is always sweet. I had worked extra hard to keep our sales up in order to pay invoices on time. It wasn't easy. I was blessed and lucky to have a very talented and dedicated group of employees, including our sales team, tailors, and office staff. Our focus was always on the positive, and we poured out the best customer service for our loyal supporters. Our Monday morning employee meetings centered on fresh new ideas to create more business and make sure our store was attractive and interesting with lots of "buy appeal." I coached our employees on professional selling techniques so we would be at the top of our game with every opportunity. We were flying high in spite of one engine missing. I was smiling, positive and happy on the outside, and scared to death on the inside.

One of my "busy projects" that kept me going was a major production of the first of several spring style shows, the likes of which this area had never seen. The Cat & Fiddle Supper Club, located about eight miles from New Ulm in a country setting, would host it. The facility had a dinner theater with a stage, runway and a balcony, perfect for our event. The décor was heavy with red, gold and glitzy figurines. The theater had a seating capacity of about 250 people. The owner was an eccentric and wealthy lady by the name of Irene Fayne Peterson who also owned several area beauty shops.

Irene and her husband, Walt, originally built the facility to construct floats for parades for companies and individuals all over the United States. Later on, the building was converted to the supper club and dinner theater.

Irene was the owner, but Verna ran the show! The first time I met Verna she told me how the world really works, in no uncertain terms. She was small, handy and straight forward, with a passion to protect the lady boss and her turf at the Cat & Fiddle. Verna and I became great friends through the years as we continued our series of shows.

This year's show would be really special as we teamed up with Pink's (ladies store) and Tom Lindemann's Music Store. The Music store organized a band for introductory and

**Smiley Wiltscheck and the band played for dancing at our
"Expressions of Spring" style show**

background music, and for the dance that would follow. Our guest model was Viking's football star Bob "The Benchwarmer" Lurtsema. Several other Vikings players were celebrity models in future year's shows. We had a social hour, a dinner, a terrific style show, and a dance that followed. It was a sell-out and a fantastic success. To everyone in the New Ulm market, things seemed great at the Leuthold & Jensen store. Spring had begun, and Easter was around the corner.

The Easter season in 1978 meant new men's suits, ladies dresses, children's shoes and bonnets for Easter Sunday. It was a very busy time for our store, and all of the New Ulm men's clothing businesses. I was at the store Saturday morning when Konnie called, asking me to meet her at Eichten's Shoe Store at about 10:00 to help pick out new shoes for our children. As soon as I could get a break at about 9:45, I left the store and told my guys, "I'll be right back."

In a hurry to help my wife pick out our children's new Easter shoes, I hustled out the front door. I was chewing gum and not wanting to throw it on the sidewalk, I walked over to a garbage receptacle at the corner just down the street to dispose of it. As I leaned over to throw away my gum, I noticed that it was full of black plastic suit hangers. Being a thrifty retailer, my first thought was, "Boy, they cost money; I should pull them out and reuse them." I also noticed that the the store's name had been scraped off. Maybe someone moved out of an upper-floor apartment and discarded the hangers. I headed into Eichten's to help with the family shoe purchases, but kept thinking about the hangers. Richard "Duke" Eicthen was a charismatic raspy-voiced retailer who ran and owned one of the most

"Seek role models. It's the pioneers who get all the arrows. Role models; study them, copy them, compete with them and try to surpass them."

successful shoe stores in Minnesota. He was helping Konnie with the shoes. "How's business, Jim?" he asked me.

"It's been busy," I replied. I always liked Duke Eichten, who was one of the first New Ulm businessmen to make me feel really welcomed when I came to New Ulm. I would seek advice from him during my early years of building my business.

Our four children (Christopher, Amy, Eric and Sarah) were there with Konnie, sitting in the red vinyl fitting chairs waiting their turn to slip into a new pair of shoes. It would be white patent leather for the girls and black oxfords for the boys. Eichten's was swamped with customers since tomorrow was Easter Sunday. As we pondered our choices for the kids, my mind kept going back to the hangers in the garbage. Why would anyone throw away good hangers?

After getting the new shoes purchased and saying good-bye to my family, I headed back to the store. As I crossed the street, I headed back to the garbage receptacle where I'd seen the hangers. I scooped up an armful of hangers and took them back to my store. Steve Jacobson was selling a handsome sport coat and slack combination to one of our regular customers. "What the heck are your doing with the hangers?" I dumped them on my desk in back and proceeded to help wait on our customers.

A bit later as I sat at my desk, I picked up one of the rescued hangers thinking, "How wasteful to throw away good usable hangers, these things cost money." As I turned one of the hangers over, I was thinking, "These are the same as we use, and why would someone go to the trouble to scrape off the labels? Why would someone waste their time doing that? Maybe they were trying to hide something. Could this have something to do with my missing clothing?" It was not a good day to sit and reflect on used hangers. We were having a great business day. Jim Brand had just made a nice sale to some people from Springfield. Springfield, Minnesota was one of my best sources of loyal customers and near the farm where I was raised. "Mouse," as we called him, got that nickname since we had more than one Jim working at the store, and because he was such an industrious young worker, scurrying about like a little mouse. Jim was a high school student and former neighbor kid. I met him when we moved into our house on West Street. He was an energetic, smart and very personable young man. Jim Brand recently recalled his days working at the store; he reminded me of how busy we were, and how we would sell sweaters and other items right out of the box before we had time to get them priced and inventoried. Those were the fun and crazy days of retailing. Jim comes from a great family. His parents, Don and Myrtle, are most remarkable. Don is a retired sports writer and radio personality. Myrtle is a stay-at-home mom who raised two sets of twins, eight children in all. Myrtle would make pies in a fashion that resembled a factory assembly line. They were to die for. She often brought a sample to our store. The Brands are all bright, caring and giving people. They have done so much for the community of New Ulm in so many ways. They are the first ones at your door if you are in need. Jim, one of the twins, is, as they say, a natural-born salesman. Jim and his family were wonderful neighbors and very good friends. He was one of the best salesmen I ever had. So was Steve Jacobson. I have been blessed with wonderful employees throughout my entire business career.

"What's the deal with the hangers, Jens?" Steve asked.

"I'm not sure; they were in the garbage can, just down the street. Steve, I'm just wondering if these hangers could have anything to do with our missing clothing, and what else might be in that garbage can."

Steve jumped to his feet "I'll go check it out. I'll be right back." He returned a few minutes later with more hangers, and a brown paper bag.

Steve slowly opened the partially torn bag someone had crumpled up and thrown away. Dumping the contents on my desk, we examined the items including an assortment of labels and tags that had been removed from

Sales team: Steve Jacobson, Jim Brand, Steve Burns, Jamie Towner, Don Piepenburg and me

men's clothing. All these clues related back to our store, our brands and our merchandise. Some were embroidered labels that had apparently been cut out of suit coats, jackets and topcoats. I could feel my face getting red as I began to feel sick. Was this the break we were looking for? Was this the clue to the mysterious and long-drawn-out theft of our merchandise? What else was in the garbage container?

As we continued to dig through the tags, we found things with Fred Meine Clothing and Fred Meine, Jr.'s name on them. Steve and I looked at each other and gasped, Fred? No, I thought to myself, it can't be, but the garbage receptacle is on the corner just down from his store, and the labels were mixed in with Fred's notes and other mail, plus, I always felt there was something suspicious about Fred. Now I was becoming convinced that he may well be the one stealing merchandise from our store.

I told Steve to keep this confidential until we know for sure what is going on. "I'll call Police Chief Richard Gulden and see what we should do and how to proceed." My hands were shaking as I dialed the number to the New

Ulm Police Department. I knew the Chief of Police quite well so I asked for him. Chief Gulden was out of town for the Easter weekend so I talked to Cpl. Douglas Wiesner about my findings in the garbage, and my suspicion that my business neighbor Fred Meine, Jr. may be involved.

"You aren't finished when you are defeated; you are finished when you quit."

— *Harvey Mackay*

Chapter 8
Suspect Number One

C pl. Douglas Wiesner asked me to come to the station, about a block away from my store at 14 North Minnesota Street to discuss my concerns. Entering the main door, I asked a young female receptionist if I could speak to Cpl. Wiesner.

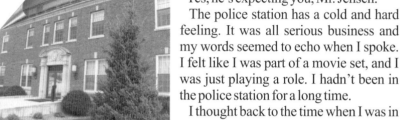

"Yes, he's expecting you, Mr. Jensen."

The police station has a cold and hard feeling. It was all serious business and my words seemed to echo when I spoke. I felt like I was part of a movie set, and I was just playing a role. I hadn't been in the police station for a long time.

I thought back to the time when I was in second grade in country school, our entire school took a ride on the 400 Train from Sleepy Eye to New Ulm, about fourteen miles. We toured the city with our teacher, Mrs. Lendt, and saw its sights. We were in awe of the Herman Monument; we toured Eibner's Restaurant, KNUJ Radio, and The Journal newspaper office, ending up visiting the police station, and stepping into an empty jail cell.

The former police station, now City Hall

Today was a serious trip, I felt light headed and nervous. I walked into Cpl. Wiesner's office and he greeted me with a very professional, "Hello, Mr. Jensen." It almost seemed like he was positioning himself for a battle, and didn't want to let our friendship or personalities get involved. "Sit down, Jim," he said to me, as he gestured to an uncomfortable-looking oak chair near his desk. "Tell me what makes you think Fred Meine, Jr. is involved is some sort of crime against you?"

I briefed Wiesner on what had been happening to our business for the past three years, including the mysterious missing merchandise and the inventory/audit concerns. "I think you'll be interested in what I found today in the garbage receptacle." I said. I relayed to him the events of the day centering on the garbage receptacle, and what Steve and I discovered.

I asked Cpl. Wiesner if he had a key to open the garbage container in order to empty the entire contents to see what else was in there. He assured me they did, and he would have it emptied, and asked me to call him back later in the day.

At the store, I waited to see what else the officers might discover in the trash container. About an hour later, Cpl. Wiesner called and asked if I could come back to the station to meet with him. We looked over the contents that they had just retrieved and found various clothing tickets and brand name tags that had been taken off clothing such as shirts, ties, suits etc. As we continued to go through the contents, we found a brown book wrapper with the mailing label of Fred Meine, Jr., P.O. Box 293, New Ulm, Minnesota. There were other receipts and letters all referencing Fred Meine, Jr., the Fred Meine Clothing store or his residence. More and more I became convinced about his involvement as we continued to sort through the large pile of tags, labels, and more hangers.

The names on the clothing tags were brands that only our store carried in New Ulm. When we completed going through the garbage, pulling out everything that we felt we needed, Cpl. Wiesner asked me if I had any idea how this clothing could be getting out of the store. I told him I really had no idea, but that we had done a security check some time ago and did everything we possibly could do to make sure the building was secure. After listening to my story, Wiesner said, "Jim, let's walk over to your store. I want to take a look around to see if I can discover the point of illegal entry."

After walking through our building, Cpl. Wiesner discovered the following: There were only four possible ways anyone could get into the building. It would have to be 1) through the heavy wooden door in the basement connecting the Leuthold Jensen and Meine store, 2) through the front door customer entrance, 3) through the back door or, 4) through the windows in the back. He studied all these places "with a fine tooth comb," finding nothing that might have been disturbed or tampered with. It appeared to Wiesner that our building was secure. Someone must have access to store keys or some other unknown means of entry.

The area in the basement where the common door to Meine's was located appeared to be undisturbed and foolproof with bars and locks securely in place. Various old racks, shelving and discarded fixtures were stored there. The windows had heavy steel bars, and the doors on the main floor had secure locks that had been changed recently with new keys. Doug Wiesner said in his report: "At this time we just couldn't come up with an answer as to where or how Mr. Meine could be getting into Mr. Jensen's store." Cpl. Wiesner stated "Since the store was busy, and I didn't want to draw attention to the situation, we decided to wait until the store closed at 5:00 and then meet and decide what to do from there."

Chapter 9
The Plot Thickens

Now my Danish temper was really getting hot. Was this person who was supposed to be a friendly competitor really stealing my clothing inventory? I just couldn't imagine it. I was very tense and nervous about what was happening, and I needed to bring Konnie into the loop. I went home to think it all through and talk with my wife about what had just transpired, and tell her I would be staying late so Officer Wiesner could come back for another look at our buildings. I told Konnie about finding the hangers and the evidence in the garbage containers and my suspicions about Fred's involvement. Konnie just couldn't believe it. "Are you really convinced Fred has something to do with the missing inventory"

"Yes, I'm serious; I think he has everything to do with it," I answered.

Konnie just couldn't picture Fred as a dishonest person. "I know," I responded "and Hazel Meine (Fred's sister and the New Ulm Chamber of Commerce Executive Secretary) is so nice and such a good friend. If it is true, it would devastate her."

Hazel Meine, Fred's sister

I met Hazel Meine after I began working for Hugo Neubauer at the Leuthold Neubauer clothing store in downtown New Ulm in 1966. At the suggestion of my boss, I went to the Chamber of Commerce office to introduce myself. The Chamber office, at that time was just across the street, and up a very steep staircase that led to the office. I was winded from the long, steep climb, but this may have been the most important meeting of my business career. The receptionist welcomed me; it was the first time I met Mary Ellen Domeier. She was employed by the Chamber as an assistant to Hazel Meine.

Later on and throughout my years as a businessman, I would spend countless hours on committees and boards working with Mary Ellen. She is one of New Ulm's most gifted and brightest individuals. Mary Ellen went on to have a very successful career in banking, including serving as the first women to be elected as President of the Minnesota Bankers Association. As I write this book, Mary Ellen is still active as Board Chair of Bank Midwest and serving her community on various boards and as a volunteer to many organizations.

That same day, Mary Ellen and Hazel both encouraged me to become involved with the Chamber. I became very involved as the years went by and would spend many hours visiting and working with Hazel Meine. She had a dry sense of humor and a very charming demeanor. I really liked and admired Hazel. She truly loved her work and did a wonderful job of promoting our city and our businesses. Hazel was a visionary who had a passion for making New Ulm a better place, and was a friend to all of the business people.

After leaving my home and driving down Broadway Street, heading for downtown New Ulm, I pondered the possibility of Fred Meine, Jr.'s involvement, and the fact that his sister was such a special person. I struggled to keep it all in perspective. The store was busy, and I needed to get back and help my customers so they would look their best for Easter Sunday. So many thoughts raced through my mind.

After parking my car, I intentionally walked by Fred's store and paused to peer into his display windows. It was hard to see into his store because his store windows had old-fashioned green and yellow shades to protect his display garments from fading. As I strained to look into his store, I saw what I believed to be a Johnny Carson brand suit on display about half way to the back of his store. Johnny Carson suits were one of the best-selling brands that we had—and I was certain Fred Meine Jr. would not have this brand in his store. It was a light tan suit with white topstitching. The brand name was Johnny Carson Apparel, made by the M. Wile Suit Company of Buffalo, New York. I'd sold many of these suits, and I just knew this suit in his store was my property. At this point there was little doubt in my mind that Fred Meine, Jr. was the mysterious thief. But how was he getting into my store, and how much of my inventory does he have?

I was so upset I just had to tell someone what I had just seen. Steve Jacobson almost choked when I told him about the suit. He said let's go in and confront him and see what he has to say. "Well, Steve, I don't want to do or say something that we might regret later."

About that same time I received a phone call from Cpl. Wiesner who informed me that in order to obtain a search warrant to go into Meine's store, we would need proof that there is a piece of clothing in his store that belongs to us. Wiesner had contacted Jim Olson, Assistant Brown County Attorney, who told Wiesner that basically what we had was circumstantial evidence. We would need to have someone purchase an item from Meine Clothing, and then positively identify that item as our property. I excitedly passed along the information to Wiesner that I was sure I had just seen a suit on display, just barely in sight near the back of Fred's store. I was almost positive it was our property. Now I needed a way to get the evidence that we needed to solve this mystery.

"Every accomplishment begins with the decision to try."

— Harvey Mackay

Chapter 10

The Suit Purchase

Who could I ask to go into Meine's to make the purchase that would give us positive proof that Fred had our merchandise? Who could I ask to do such a favor, and who could I trust to keep it confidential?

Eldon and Carolyn Traulich were friends. They owned the trailer court that we lived in when we moved to New Ulm. A twelve by sixty-foot trailer was the first home we owned in New Ulm. They became customers and social friends.

Eldon was a tall and lanky guy who needed a special suit size that most stores don't carry—an extra long, for men usually over six foot-three inches tall. We did carry a few. Eldon and Carolyn had moved to New Ulm from the lake country in northern Minnesota. They were hard working, honest and very likeable. A week or two earlier, Eldon came into my store to shop and look at my extra-long suit selection. He found one he really liked—one of the new Johnny Carson three-piece spring suits that featured white topstitching on the lapels and pockets. He wanted to come back to try it on when his wife could come with him.

About a week later they returned to the store to purchase the suit. When I went to the rack to select the suit that Eldon had tried on, it had vanished, and no one remembered selling it. This all came back to me when I saw what I thought was the same suit in Fred Maine's store just a half an hour ago. Maybe he had stolen that suit from me.

Could I ask Eldon Traulich go over to Fred's store and see if the suit that was missing was in Fred's store? When I called, he came in just a few minutes. Maybe he could sense I was desperate. I told Eldon the whole story of the mystery of the missing inventory, and that we suspected Fred may be involved. Of course, he was shocked. Eldon was hardly able to believe the whole bizarre story, but was willing to help out. He went to Meine's to go suit shopping, and brought back startling news!

Eldon returned to my store to report on what happened at Meine's store. When Eldon asked Fred for the type and size suit he was looking for, Fred said he thought he had it in his "storage area," and would go get it for him. Fred brought up the same suit Eldon had recently tried on in our store. Eldon also noticed that as he opened up the jacket in front of the mirror, it had no labels inside the jacket, and that he could see the needle holes where the label would normally be.

Eldon had done me a big favor, and I thanked him, telling him he would probably hear from the New Ulm Police Department shortly. To this day, I appreciate and admire the courage it took for Eldon to help us out, knowing he would end up getting involved much more than he probably would have liked. I believe he did it because he felt it was the right thing to do. I will always be grateful to Eldon for what he did in helping us solve our mystery.

I called Cpl. Wiesner at his residence after I discovered he had left the office for the day. During our phone conversation, I told him I thought we had some good news that might help us with the evidence we needed to get a search warrant. I explained the details of story of Eldon Traulich finding the same suit at Meine's he had tried on at my store. Cpl. Wiesner was confident we may have something with this discovery, and that it could be what we needed to obtain a search warrant.

"What sets you apart is what gets you ahead."

— *Harvey Mackay*

Chapter 11
Hidden in Plain Sight

Cpl. Wiesner asked Jim Olson, the Brown County Attorney, to come to the station to discuss the situation with him, Eldon Traulich and me.

Attorney Olson asked me to recap the general background of the events leading up to today's findings. As I did a review of events, Cpl. Wiesner also displayed the contents that were found in the garbage receptacle in front of Meine's store.

In order to better understand the process of obtaining a search warrant, Olson explained that the only items that can be seized from a search warrant are those items specifically listed in the warrant, and any items of contraband that the officers know or believe to be contraband.

We then discussed the idea of buying the suit from Meine so there would be no question where it came from. This would also give us time to examine the suit for positive identification. Eldon Traulich agreed to purchase the suit. He called his wife Carolyn and asked her to bring their checkbook and meet him at the Meine store. Cpl. Wiesner and I chatted about going back to my store to examine the portals of entry one more time to see how Meine was gaining entry to our store. Wiesner was to follow later so we would not be seen together to avoid suspicion.

A few minutes later, Eldon Traulich stopped at the police station to tell Wiesner that Fred Meine Jr. had closed for the day, and so he was not able to purchase the suit. He would try again on Monday morning.

Wiesner met me at my store right before closing time. Once the store was empty of customers, Cpl. Wiesner, Steve Jacobson and I went through the store, focused on looking for a possible point of entry. We were unable to locate any point on the main floor so we went to the basement under the newest part of the store. We checked everything, and when we got to the door between our store and the Meine store, we checked every crack in the door.

After looking for any "thread of evidence" for months and years, we finally found what had haunted me: The secret to where and how Fred Meine, Jr. was getting access to my building and my inventory! After all the years of frustration, we finally found it; the mystery was solved! The door was divided into four panels. After examining the big heavy door over and over again, Wiesner was kneeling down close to the floor and noticed something suspicious. The bottom right panel had some marks on it that appeared to be new and fresh. With his police flashlight, Wiesner examined the panel closely. What he discovered was that one of the recessed panels had been finely cut along the inside edge. He now could see all four sides where it had been cut through, and when we pushed on it, it moved a little. We tried to see if we could pull the panel out or move it, but we couldn't. Somehow it was fastened on the other side. With the flashlight, we could see there were pieces of metal that appeared to be hinges on the top.

The bathroom door Meine practiced on before cutting the panel in the door between our stores

After studying the door panel, Wiesner said, " Jim, there's no doubt in my mind now that Fred Meine, Jr. is stealing your inventory and gaining access through this hole in the door." All three of us stood silently staring at the door. Now it seemed so obvious; how could we have looked at it so many times and yet missed it? There it was, literally hidden in plain sight.. At that point my surge of adrenalin kicked in. I wanted to confront Fred Meine, Jr., and demand answers and get my property back.

Looking into Meine's store basement from the Jensen Clothing side

Before we left the store, we noticed a drilled hole in one of the large wooden beams near the ceiling that separated the basements. It appeared that it had been used for water pipes years ago. Steve got on a ladder, shined the flashlight into Fred's basement and peeked through the hole. What Steve saw was a basement filled with our clothing. "My gosh Jens he has a bunch of clothes hanging in there and they look like ours."

It was the first glance at the many things we would find that had been missing from our store. We were glad to finally know how Meine was getting into our store—but at the same time sick to think that a neighbor and fellow businessman would be capable of such a crime. My head was swimming with many thoughts, and how to handle all the things that were about to happen.

Wiesner suggested that Steve and I do a quick inventory to try to determine, to the best of our ability, what was missing from our store. Steve and I agreed that we would come back to the store later and begin doing the inventory. This would promise to be a long and stressful weekend.

I called Ron O'Brien at his home in Albert Lea and told him of the findings, and that we had discovered who was stealing our inventory, and how he was getting into the store. He was shaken, as we were, that Fred would do this. "Jim, I just can't believe your neighbor is stealing your merchandise from you, and then selling it? I've never heard of a retailer stealing from his competitor; especially your next-door neighbor. It sounds like the craziest story I've ever heard."

I was in disbelief myself. I told Ron I would call him Monday morning and let him know when we found out more, and the details as to how we would proceed. Even though we had discovered the point of illegal entry, we still needed Fred to sell the suit to Eldon Traulich Monday morning in order to have the evidence to obtain the search warrant we would need. Ron assured me that he would stay in the office and be available on a moment's notice.

Fred Meine, Jr. had stolen a lot of my clothing inventory, and now we knew exactly how he was getting into my store. What I didn't know is why he would do it to me? What had I done that would make him commit these crimes? I closed my eyes, trying to imagine Fred crawling through that hole in the middle of the night to steal our clothing. This was a creepy and disgusting picture in my mind. I was worried what the public reaction would be to all of this, but I couldn't get down on myself. I had to stay confident and composed.

"Plenty of people are willing to beat you; don't beat yourself"

— Harvey Mackay

Chapter 12
Late Night Inventory

By now I had informed Konnie of the newest findings. She now knew, as I did, that there was no question that Fred had been stealing from us. It was just—how long and how much?

"Well, so much for bringing him cookies and brownies and trying to be a good neighbor," Konnie lamented.

She was concerned that Fred might come into the store while Steve and I were taking the inventory. I saw a little humor in what she said, thinking "Would he (Fred) be surprised!" I could just picture it: Fred crawling through the hole and looking up and seeing Steve and me standing there. OOPS! Anyway, I kissed my wife goodnight and reminded her it would be a long evening. The next day was Easter Sunday, so I would help her hide the Easter baskets of candy for our four kids when I got home. Our children loved to get up Easter morning and hunt for their baskets; when they would find them, I would help them sort through the candy, and of course, sample my favorites.

I jumped into my grey and black Ford pickup truck and headed to Steve's house. This was going to be a long night. It had been an unusually warm March, but tonight was chilly with a grey, foggy mist in the air sending a shiver through my tired body. I switched on the windshield wipers to clear my vision; the night was dark and dreary. Steve was such a great guy; I always could count on him. Tonight I felt more comfortable having Steve (who we often called Jake) with me just in case Fred would show up. I had told him to tell his wife Gay what was going on so she would understand why we had to be at the store tonight. She just shook her head. "I can't believe this is happening."

"I know," I said, "but at least we know where our clothing has been going." Jake came out with a bag of snacks Gay made to keep us going; I laughed and said, "This isn't a picnic, Jake."

"That's okay, if you don't want any of the pickles Gay sent, I'll just eat them myself." Steve knew that I loved pickles, especially Gay's pickles. One night after going to Mankato to a movie we ended up at their home. Steve and I were in their basement playing a game of pool. While there, I discovered

Gay's stash of delicious dill pickles and devoured the best part of a whole jar. We laughed about the pickles, and we talked about our families and our friendship as we drove to the store. We parked the truck down the street in front of Mowan's Bar so Fred wouldn't get tipped off that we were going into the store. We quietly entered the store and began to organize our plan of attack on the quick inventory. It was eerie, every time the old building would creak or any noise occurred, we would jump in response.

After an hour or so of taking the inventory, Jake and I decided to go to the basement and look into Fred's basement once more to see how much merchandise of ours he had stashed. We got our courage up and tiptoed to the stairway, I could feel my heart pounding in the dark. Slowly we descended the basement steps, flashlights in hand. Walking close for mutual support, we made our way to the back of the room. Steve climbed up the ladder that we had left against the stone wall. He took another look through the drilled hole. Shaking his head in disbelief, Steve handed me the flashlight. "Jim, you better take a look for yourself."

The basement that Fred used to hide our stolen inventory

Spying through the peep hole, I got a knot in my stomach when I realized the magnitude of what was happening, and how it would affect our lives and our business. Steve and I went back upstairs and finished our work. It was very late when we left for home and some needed rest.

After dropping Steve off, I pulled into my garage and turned off the engine. I sat in my truck and thought: How the heck did I get into this mess;

why me? I closed my eyes and said a prayer for strength and courage to see this through, and to do it honestly with dignity. I needed to protect the business interest of the Leuthold Company and our family. Quietly entering the house, I noticed a note: *Dear Jim, It was getting late, so I hid the baskets. Love, Konnie.*

Exhausted and weary, it felt good to be next to my beautiful wife, away from my troubles at the store. Even though I had a lot on my mind, I was totally mentally and physically exhausted, and fell asleep knowing that with motivation and determination, I would keep focused on resolving this whole matter that was looming.

"Ability is what you're capable of doing. Motivation determines what you do. Attitude determines how well you do it"

— *Harvey Mackay*

Chapter 13
Easter Sunday

Sunday morning was Easter Sunday. The kids got up early, not knowing the storm that was brewing in my business. Dressed in our Easter clothes, we went to the First United Methodist Church at Center and Broadway Street, just a block from the store. We were a little late and the main sanctuary was full, so our family sat upstairs in the balcony. The Reverend Lowell Reinking led us in a beautiful worship service. I was a nervous wreck and kept getting up and pacing around while I tried to imagine what Monday would bring. After the service ended, the congregation went to the parking lot where we released balloons signifying the risen Christ. In spite of everything that was looming at the store, we had a wonderful Easter dinner and enjoyed the day with our family.

The First United Methodist Church in New Ulm

Cpl. Wiesner agreed that we would meet again on Sunday evening to return to the garbage container to empty it once more; looking for anything else that may have been put in there over the weekend that might be considered as additional evidence. I arrived at the station at 8:00 p.m. The plan was for me to bring a copy of the inventory Steve and I had taken Saturday night, noting items we believed were missing from our store. Wiesner and I would review the list and identify tags and labels that matched any of the missing items. And that's what we did.

When we had analyzed the apparently missing inventory list, Cpl. Wiesner and I got into his personal car and drove to the garbage container. The downtown was quiet, as we knew it would be. Just a few people were walking and window-shopping in the cool early evening, enjoying their Easter Sunday. Wiesner opened his door, got out and pulled out the garbage can. When he emptied the contents into a cardboard box, we could see lots of clothing tags, some with the Leuthold Jensen name pre-printed on them, and other papers and envelopes identifying Meine Clothing and Fred Meine, Jr.

Back at the station, we combed through the garbage to extract the evidence. We talked about what we found and assumed one of two possible things were happening: Either the clothing tags we had been finding were being disposed of as the clothing was taken or they were being discarded a little bit at a time. We agreed that there wasn't any more that could be done that night, and now all we could do was wait until morning to see if Mr. Meine would sell the suit to Eldon Traulich. Once that was done, we would talk with attorney Olson about drawing up a search warrant.

"The way to become truly useful is to seek the best that other brains have to offer. Use them to supplement your own, and be prepared to give credit to them when they have helped."

— *Gordon Dean*

Chapter 14
The Last Sale

onday morning, Eldon and Carolyn Traulich parked in front of the Fred Meine Clothing Store. They walked to the front of Fred's store and paused a few minutes looking at the window display. Now they were ready to go into the store. Fred Meine had no reason to believe this was a "set up."

Fred was sitting near the back of his store on a padded chair, as was his custom. He was somewhat portly, about average height and in his late fiftys. That day he was dressed in a suit and tie. He peered through his black-rimmed glasses to see who

The location of Meine's storefront (today)

had entered his store. He got up from his chair and walked toward the Traulichs. Fred recognized Eldon and greeted him. Eldon told Fred that he wanted to show his wife the suit he tried on Saturday. Fred nodded as he put his hand to the side of his face recalling the suit he had shown to Eldon Traulich just a couple of days before. He slowly walked to the back of the store and retrieved the suit, bringing it to the front of the store where the Traulichs waited.

Fred helped his customer slip into the suit jacket; Eldon took a quick glance at the lining and noticed needle holes where the labels had been removed. Eldon asked his wife what she thought of the suit. She liked the suit and suggested that they buy it, reminding Eldon how hard it was for him to find extra longs.

After more conversation about the color, size and fit, Fred

suggested they mark the suit for the needed alterations. Eldon told him that he would need to have it altered rather quickly since they had an upcoming trip planned, and he would want to take it with him. Fred rang up the sale on an antique manually operated National Cash Register.

Eldon and Carolyn left the store with their purchase that would be the spark that would light a huge fire of news, gossip, rumors and speculation in the next few days on Minnesota Street in New Ulm—the likes of which we may never had heard before.

Eldon Traulich had been instructed to go straight to the New Ulm Police station as soon as he completed the suit purchase. Eldon parked the car on First North Street. He was on the side of the building that housed the city offices and the police station. With his new suit in hand, he walked up the steps and pulled the door open. At exactly 9:30 a.m. Monday morning he was escorted directly into the meeting room where he would report to Cpl. Wiesner and the Chief of Police, Richard Gulden.

After examining the contents of his purchase and getting a verbal report from Eldon Traulich, the police impounded the jacket and vest, along with the receipt as evidence. Cpl. Wiesner called my store and asked me to come over to verify that this was my missing merchandise. I rushed out the door and ran all the way to the police station. I examined the suit in every detail possible and was certain this was my property. I also told Wiesner that, prior to coming to the police station, I called the Johnny Carson Company (M. Wile Co.) of Buffalo, New York to check whether they ever sold any merchandise to the Meine Clothing Company or Fred Meine Jr. They told me they had never done any business with him or his store, and said that they would send a written statement to that effect. I had to do my homework to be positive we had all the details correct and in order.

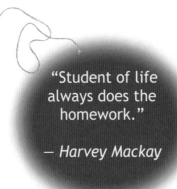

"Student of life always does the homework."

— Harvey Mackay

Chapter 15
The Search Warrant

Cpl. Wiesner called Brown County Attorney, Jim Olson, to report on what had just occurred. Jim asked Wiesner and me to come to his office to discuss the situation with him as he prepared the second page of the search warrant. The process of typing the warrant began about 10.30 a.m. I arrived at the County Attorney's office at 11:15 a.m. and at approximately 12:05 p.m., the search warrant was ready to be signed by a judge.

Attorney Olson informed us that there was a bar association luncheon at the Kaiserhoff, so we would have to go there to find a judge. Mr. Olson, Cpl. Wiesner and Spec. Blomquist did so and found Judge Moriarty at the meeting and asked him to come out to the hall area of the restaurant to read the warrant. Upon reading it, he asked "Are you sure?" They assured the judge that it was all true and factual, and he then signed it. Wiesner told Olson the police would be executing the warrant around 2 p.m.

Living in a small city like New Ulm means everyone knows almost instantly about anything "big" that happens. I knew there would be a whirlwind of phone calls, gossip and self-edited stories of everyone's opinion on what was going on at the Meine Clothing Company and how Leuthold Jensen Clothiers was involved.

Bracing for the onslaught of questions I'd soon be getting, I found refuge in my office. I pulled out my well-worn copy of the New Ulm Rural Telephone Company (now NU-Telecom) phone book. I needed to consult a lawyer to make sure I didn't do or say the wrong thing, and to protect the store's interest in the stolen inventory. I tucked the piece of paper with the phone number written on it into my shirt pocket, and later on that evening I called New Ulm attorney Bob Halvorson.

I always liked Bob. He was an excellent lawyer and as a side business, he owned and operated a grain farm. He enjoyed spending time there helping with the farm work when he could slip away from the law office. I guess we were both farm boys at heart.

I called Bob's office and he told me to come over right away.

After listening to my long explanation of the situation, Bob leaned back in his chair, gave me his usual big smile and said, "Wow."

I knew I was in good hands with Bob. He was a friend and great suit customer. When he would need a new suit, Bob would call me and let me know he was coming in. I would lay out four or five of my best-quality and best-looking suits in his size, along with several choices of coordinating shirts, ties and sox. Bob would come in and pick out one or two suits and just say, "Jim, you know what my measurements are, go ahead and alter them and pick out the shirts and ties. Call me when they are ready to be picked up." That happened many times. I love to sell suits!

> " It was hard for me to sit quietly and not shout the words to Fred Meine, Jr. that were inside me; I had to let the officers do the talking, and keep silent for now. "

Monday morning I contacted Ron O'Brien and brought him up to speed as to what would be taking place; he was already on the way to New Ulm. A few of the Leuthold store managers were coming to New Ulm as well, to give me moral support. We all gathered later that day in my store office. The whole process now was in the hands of the Brown County Attorney's office and the New Ulm Police Department who asked me to stay out of the way, and keep a cool head. It wasn't easy! I had a lot of pent-up anger and frustration. I knew the world of Fred Meine, Jr. was about to come crashing down, and all hell was about to break loose.

Before executing the search warrant, Sgt. Schapekahm, Spec. Blomquist and Cpl. Wiesner came to my store to discuss specifically which items listed on the search warrant should be looked for. The atmosphere was tense, like the lull before the storm. I was nervous and anxious to get it over with. The officers were serious and very professional in conducting their work. Part of the plan would be for Sgt. Schapekahm to stay with Meine while Officers Blomquist and Wiesner conducted the search. They left to go back to the police station to "re-group."

A little later, while visiting with the Leuthold Company managers, we discussed the concerns of protecting our interest and that of the Leuthold

Company in the form of a possible civil lawsuit. Ron O'Brien, Don Fencl and Keith Galles from the other Leuthold stores voiced their opinions about the possible outcome, and what we could do to be prepared. We also discussed how to address with the media and our customers about what had happened.

I noticed the New Ulm Police cruiser slowly roll by the front of my store windows— no flashing lights or sirens. The officers squad car quietly pulled up to the curb in front of Meine Clothing. It was hard for me to sit quietly and not shout the words to Fred Meine, Jr. that were inside me; I had to let the officers do the talking, and keep silent for now.

Chapter 16

Surprise Visitors

At 2 p.m. Officers Wiesner, Schapkahm and Blomquist arrived at the Meine Clothing Store. The New Ulm Police officers entered the store and marched in a sort of cadence as the sound of their leather-soled shoes echoed, hitting the hard wood floor. The officers found Mr. Meine sitting on a table next to the cash register. Meine's dimly lit store was empty of customers. Wiesner introduced himself and the other two officers. Cpl. Wiesner informed Fred Meine, Jr. that the reason the police officers were at his store was because they had, in their possession, a suit that had been purchased in his store which they believed to be stolen. Cpl. Wiesner also told Meine they also had reason to believe that there were other items of clothing in the store which were stolen and listed on the search warrant which they had presented to him.

After informing Fred Meine, Jr. of why they were there, Cpl. Wiesner advised him of his rights in the form of the Miranda. When asked if he understood the Miranda, he indicated "yes," and nodded yes to the question as to his willingness to answer any question they might ask concerning the matter at hand. Fred showed no emotion or signs of surprise as to what was being suggested. He never got up from his seat. At this point, the officers asked Meine to sign the Miranda form and waiver, which he did. It was witnessed by the three New Ulm Police officers present.

Cpl. Wiesner then asked Mr. Meine if he would cooperate with them and informed him that if he should try to interfere with them they would take the necessary action to prevent his interference. Fred replied, "Do what you have to do."

At this point, the word that a New Ulm Police car had parked in front of Meine's and three policemen had entered the store was spreading like crazy through the downtown. A group of citizens were looking into the windows of the Meine store. Cpl. Wiesner asked Mr. Meine if he would lock the front door so there wouldn't be any disturbance once they began the search for the missing inventory. At this point Fred said, "Sure, I could do that," and got up, slowly walking to the front door, and locked it.

Fred went behind his counter and pulled out an old faded sign that he was about to put in his window. It read, "CLOSED ALL DAY." The Meine Clothing store would never ever open again for business as usual; this was the end of an era. Fred, who walked with a limp, used his cane for support as he returned to his chair next to Officer Schapekahm. The police were anxious to see what they would find within the walls of Meine Clothing Co.

Chapter 17
The Search Begins

The search began with Cpl. Wiesner and Spec. Blomquist walking through the main floor part of the store while Meine observed them. The officers discovered several brands of suits and dress shirts in packaging with the brand name Arrow on them. I had checked with the Arrow Shirt Co. in New York and they told me that, as far back as they had records, the Meine store had never purchased any Arrow shirts from them. Cpl. Wiesner believed that all the Arrow dress shirts they had just seen (dozens of them) were stolen property. My stolen property!

The officers next decided to search the basement. As Cpl. Wiesner and Spec. Blomquist walked step by step down the heavy wooden stairway, they were astounded by the large quantity of clothing they saw hanging on pipes suspended from the ceiling and racks on the floor.

The steps to Meine's basement

Cpl. Wiesner noticed a navy blue winter jacket and, upon inspection, saw the Leuthold & Jensen label inside. He also discovered a rack of leather jackets. Cpl. Wiesner paused to consider how much they just discovered; the amount of stolen clothing was much more than he had anticipated. How could they possibly handle and inventory all of this? They then asked Fred Meine Jr. if there was clothing in his store that did not belong to him. He did not answer. Meine was starting to get agitated, not wanting to say anything more to the officers. Due to the large task before them, Cpl. Wiesner called Wm. T. O'Connor from the county attorney's office to discuss the magnitude of the project, and how to best proceed. O'Connor, known throughout southern Minnesota as a smart, excellent and tough lawyer, arrived in about fifteen minutes. O'Connor was an Irishman who was known to have a dry "tongue in cheek "sense of humor when he was out of the courtroom setting. Today he was very serious. They first talked of moving all the clothing to another location to take an inventory. However, after some discussions, they decided they must first take an inventory of what they believed to be stolen before anything could be moved.

As the search for missing clothing intensified, Cpl. Wiesner asked Meine if it was fair to say that any suit that had the labels cut out of it had been done for the purpose of hiding its identity. Mr. Meine nodded yes in response. It appeared that Fred was becoming more apprehensive while realizing the seriousness of what he had done. Later I was told that his greatest fear was that he might go to jail.

Sometime later in the day on Monday, Fred Meine, Jr. retained the services of Everett Young, Roger Hippert and Al Mueller as his legal counsel team. During the search, Spec. Blomquist asked Meine if there was clothing that should not be in his store or that did not belong to him. Meine did not answer the question. Wiesner then informed Meine that it appeared this was going to take a long time, and that if he would help, it would go faster. Meine still said nothing. The search continued late into Monday night.

Tuesday March 28th a Complaint was filed against Fred Meine, Jr. in Brown County Court by the Office of the Brown County Attorney. Meine would be charged and booked at the New Ulm Police Department on Wednesday morning. The search and seizure of the stolen merchandise continued all day Tuesday at Fred Meine's Clothing store. It was becoming an overwhelming task for the New Ulm Police.

During the day on Tuesday and for the days to come, our store was overrun with people curious about the stories that appeared in The Journal. I must admit, it was one of the strangest twists of events imaginable—having one businessman steal from his neighbor, especially in such a small town.The fact that he crawled through a secret door made it even more bizarre. It became great fodder for television and radio talk shows and the local coffee shops. Many jokes surfaced. Among them, one that people would tell was, "How did Fred choose the clothes he would steal from Leuthold Jensen's?"

The answer was, "He would go: "eeny, meeny, MEINE, moe" taking the item he stopped on." If I heard that one once, I heard it a hundred times.

The clothing that the officers were inventorying was being transported to the empty former post office building. (It would eventually become the Museum for the Brown County Historical Society.) The amount of inventory they were removing from the Meine store was incredible, and now they were beginning to run out of room at the old post office building!

Chapter 18

Charged!

The reality and consequences of what was happening smacked me in the face when I read a front page story in The Journal describing the charging of Fred Meine Jr. with the crime of possession and sales of clothing believed to be stolen from my store. The whole story was now out in the public. Everyone who read The Journal or listened to KNUJ Radio heard the reports that Fred had been arrested, charged and booked for a crime of stealing, possessing and selling men's clothing taken from my store. I was in a state of mild shock as I read what the reporters wrote and the details of what Fred had been charged with. It had become an event that was blowing up like a huge balloon, getting bigger each day; about to explode. It was so strange knowing that someone we knew as a business competitor and neighbor was apparently trying to put us out of business by sneaking into our business and stealing from us. There was that moment when I picked up *The Journal* and saw Fred's picture and wondered how this could have ever happened. How did Fred hatch up this

FRED MEINE JR.

Fred Meine, Jr. as he appeared in the New Ulm Journal

wierd idea to slither through a hole in the door and crawl into my store? I just shook my head in dis-belief; how crazy was this whole story? When I saw Fred's photograph and read the story I was disgusted thinking "people in New Ulm just don't do this kind of thing." Unfortunately, he did.

Knowing the seriousness of the criminal activity Fred Meine was accused of and charged with, I was surprised to discover that he would be released on his own recognizance, without any bail bond. I was about to learn a lot about the legal system, and how those who commit a crime, and in this specific case, seemed, in my opinion, to have the advantage.

I was trying to balance my home life, keep my business moving forward, be prepared and involved with the legal process, and answer the barrage of questions from the media, family, friends and customers. It would be a difficult challenge.

Chapter 19
The Meeting

On Wednesday, at the request of Fred Meine, Jr., a meeting was arranged between my attorney and me and Fred Meine and his attorney. I was told the meeting purpose was twofold: 1) Fred wished to "clear the air" between the two of us, and 2) To discuss authorizing me to do a walkthrough of the Meine store in order to assist the New Ulm Police Department with the difficult task they had in determining which items belonged to Leuthold Jensen's.

My attorney, Bob Halvorson, and I went to the meeting held at the Mueller Law Office. As I walked into the room, I glanced at Fred; we made eye contact and then quickly looked away. It was a very tense and uneasy situation. I was face to face with the very person whom I believed had stolen thousands of dollars of my inventory for the past three years. After the initial greeting, Fred and I never again looked at each other; it was almost is if we were invisible to each other. I wasn't too interested in "clearing the air" between us, as was suggested by Meine's attorney.

My intentions were to find out how much more of my clothing he still had in his store. I didn't come to the meeting to tell Fred I wasn't mad at him, because I was. I sat within a few feet of a person that had almost ruined my business and my life. I was very angry and upset and wanted answers. The lawyers did most of the talking and finally, it was resolved that I would be allowed to go into the Meine store and help identify my inventory in order to assist the police department in speeding up the process.

My attorney contacted Wiesner to tell him we had permission from Meine's attorney, allowing me to enter the Meine store. At 4:30 p.m., Cpl. Wiesner called attorney Al Mueller, who stated that he was with Fred and Fred's wife at that moment, and that Fred had given his written permission for me to go into his store. Cpl. Wiesner would only allow this if we were given permission directly from the Brown County Attorney's Office. Finally, at 5:00 p.m. on Wednesday, Wm T. O'Connor called, granting official permission for me and my store employees to enter the Meine's store.

This would be one of the most incredible experiences I would ever encounter. Steve Jacobsen and I left for Meine's Store with great anticipation. Little did we know what we were about to see. In the retail clothing business we get very familiar with our merchandise. We go to the clothing markets and spend long hours going through hundreds of samples, styles, brands, and colors. We wait with anticipation for the new arrivals as the seasons change. When the boxes of merchandise arrive, we are so proud and excited to show the new selections to our customers. We unpack them, put our price tags on them, and prepare them for attractive displays. Some people say that we fall in love with our merchandise— a somewhat true statement. That is, of course if you love the clothing business, which I did and do to this day.

In a small store like ours, we know our inventory like our children—now our "missing" children. It felt very strange to be going into Meine Clothing on this hunting trip. A small crowd of people gathered near the entrance of Meine's store. They were curious and shouted questions to us. We smiled and waved, not able to say anything to the customers and friends we knew so well. The onlookers gawked and strained to see into the windows that were covered for the most part by brown wrapping paper to keep it private during the search-and-seizure process.

Knocking on the heavy glass door, I got the attention of Office Chuck Raabe, who unlocked the door. Steve and I were now inside; it was uncomfortably warm in the store from the steam heat. I slipped out of my wool suit coat, hung it on a hook in the back of the store and loosened my tie. Stacks of shirts, ties, slacks and belts were piled on the tables. It was so eerie and dramatic to be in Meine's store. As we looked over the piles of clothing, we knew they were almost 100 percent our merchandise! In a strange way, we had unknowingly stocked two stores for the past three or four years. Steve walked with me as we assessed the task ahead of us; he would go the extra mile to get it done no matter how large the challenge. I knew he would.

"There's no
traffic jam on the
extra mile."

— Harvey Mackay

Chapter 20
Dreams to Nightmares

When I purchased Mr. Neubauer's interest in the Leuthold store in 1970, I dreamed of being a success and making my family proud of me. I would think back fondly to when we were kids on the farm, and we would set up a pretend store in the grove of trees right behind our farmhouse. Our dad would let us use some old boards to build shelves like those we saw when we went to Art Mogensen's store in Evan. Mom and Dad shopped for many of the basics at their store near our farm. Mom washed and saved the soup and bean cans to stock our fictional store. Black dirt and water was mixed up as mud pies to sell as well. I would pretend to be Art Mogensen and my sisters would play the roles of Art's helpers or his wife. The Mogensens were nice friendly people who had really figured out what customer service was all about back in the fifties. Dad could buy his bib overalls there; mom could buy the groceries; and we usually got a treat of some kind. I really believe these small-town business people were a strong influence on my someday owning my own retail store.

My hometown of Morgan was very robust in the mid to late 1950s. I can recall going into the Morgan Hardware store, owned by Lloyd and Edith Hopfenspirger, to look at the toys and such at Christmas time. Lloyd would patiently explain all the features of the new Red Rider BB gun that I so desperately wanted. He would take the time knowing it was more than likely not going to be a sale. These kind and gentle business owners loved and cared about their customers. They would always ask about our family and how things were going at school.

On Saturday nights during the summer, our family (all six of us) would go to town, park the car on Main Street and spend the evening socializing. I would go see a Roy Rogers or Gene Autry movie for a dime at the Morgan Theater. My Mom and Aunt Bessie would sit in the car and watch people stroll by. My sisters played in the Morgan High Band that performed in the band stand parked in the middle of Vernon Avenue, Morgan's main street. After the concert, they would go into Corral Café hoping to find their friends and probably some boys to flirt with. Main Street had at least two or three popcorn stands, with popcorn that tasted as heavenly as the smell that floated about the downtown. My Dad and Uncle Matt played cards in the smoke filled pool hall, visiting with their friends and neighbors about farming issues and politics.

These were the good old days of retailing that I'd hoped for when I bought my store in New Ulm. For the most part, it all had come true until the mysterious thefts began.

> "Believe in yourself. If you believe in yourself, well, then, there's nothing you can't accomplish. So don't ever quit."
>
> — Harvey Mackay

Now I needed to be strong and see this through, no matter how bad it would get. Konnie and I had some time to discuss what would be happening as a result of the information we had. I held my wife's hand and told her how much I loved her and how I appreciated her support and understanding. I promised her when the Fred Meine case was over, and we finished getting the store back on track, we would leave New Ulm forever. I was embarrassed that some people made fun of us for not finding out sooner what was happening to our inventory. I was sick of all the phone calls, the kidding and the jokes that people were making up about the crime. Most of all, I was crushed that someone would do such an awful thing to us when we had done them no harm. Our plan would be to move out and start all over somewhere else as soon as things were finished and business was taken care of.

Back at Meine's, it was time to continue our walk through of Fred's store. Steve Jacobson and I browsed through the store's main floor. The only merchandise that wasn't ours was very old and included derby-style hats, many still in their original boxes, some interesting jewelry consisting of cufflinks and tie clips, some western shirts, and a few shirts, suits and slacks.

What I saw in the basement was very disturbing; even after an enormous amount of clothing had been removed, a substantial number of items remained. They included rows of suits, leather coats, slacks, ties, and sweaters; all our clothing, right there in his basement! Why had Fred done this?

With the permission of Meine's attorneys and the Brown County Attorney, the police gladly accepted our offer of assistance with taking the inventory, and we went to work. Konnie, my sister Mary and my son Chris came to Meine's store to assist Steve, the police officers, and me.

The officers continued taking the inventory to the old post office building to be held as evidence until the trial. The clothing was loaded into a semi-

trailer for transport. The inventory process continued throughout the evening Wednesday. The next morning, we had completed most of it. At 5:00 a.m., we left the Meine Clothing Store and returned to our store to total up the sheets of inventory we had recorded. The total was staggering. The retail value of the stolen inventory was in excess of $170,000! I was shocked. How could a fifty-nine-year old disabled man crawl through a small paneled opening and remove that much merchandise? It couldn't be possible, could it?

Everyone went home tired, and literally passed out from stress and exhaustion. I had nightmares about what the people in New Ulm would say.

Later, New Ulm Police Officer, Chuck Raabe, commented "As we were searching the place, we found there wasn't much in Meine's that was his. It was the most unusual case I've ever been involved with." I really appreciated how hard the New Ulm Police officers worked on the case. They were so professional and did their best to be fair to everyone. I will always be thankful to Officers Wiesner, Schapekahm, Blomquist and Raabe for what they did to resolve the matter.

Chapter 21
The Legal Process

The story of Fred Meine's secret door to a free "inventory buffet" had gone nationwide. Someone saw it on the Johnny Carson late-night television show, and the National Inquirer called to interview me for a story. People sent us clippings of news stories from all over the country; many of these were from our classmates or from people who had moved from New Ulm and read the article in their area newspaper. All of a sudden it seemed as though the whole world knew about this strange and bizarre story of one clothing merchant stealing merchandise from the next-door business. It truly was one of those things that made people scratch their heads in disbelief.

The next pages include selected portions of the fascinating transcripts of the hearings that followed the charging of Fred Meine Jr. in Brown County Court. They tell of Fred switching lawyers and the beginning of a long and tough court battle. As you read the testimony, you will hear Fred Meine respond to the questions while seated in the witness stand. It also includes the

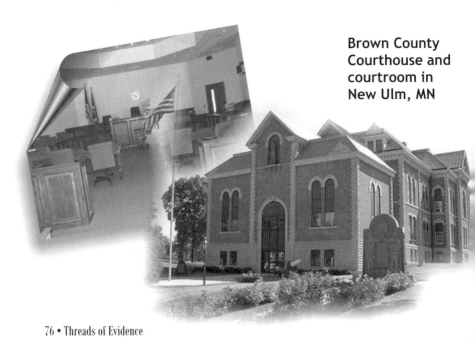

Brown County Courthouse and courtroom in New Ulm, MN

testimony of people from New Ulm and the surrounding area who became involved in the case in one way or another. Through all of this you may understand the agony we felt as the legal process gave us great concern as to whether Fred Meine Jr., would be brought to justice, and if we would regain possession of our stolen clothing.

At age thirty-three, never having been involved in any serious court case, I found myself on the brink of what would become a very publicized case debated in the courtroom at Center and State Street in New Ulm. Walking into the building, up the steps the morning of April 3, 1978, I was anxious and wishing this would be a quick process so I could take care of my business and get it all behind me. That would not happen.

Before I went in, I paused for a moment, drew a deep breath and focused on staying positive. Now ready, I opened the door to the courtroom, walked in and took a seat. It seemed as though everyone in the room was staring at me. The silence in the room was broken as the clerk said, "All Rise" as the judge entered the room and took his seat at the bench. The long-anticipated legal process was about to begin. "You may be seated."

The proceedings were now at the District Court level, and Fred was about to make his first appearance in the Fifth Judicial District Court before the Honorable Judge Noah Rosenbloom.

Fred was seated with his attorney, William Schade; the proceedings were about to begin. The courtroom was overflowing with media representatives and curious citizens. My attorney informed me that the purpose of this hearing was to present the defendant, Fred Meine, Jr. with the complaint and charges that were being filed against him.

The testimony oozes with confidence on the part of the Brown County Attorney's Office, making it sound like proving the case would be a "walk in the park." However, Bill Schade, Meine's smart and capable attorney, would make it clear that he would move to have the charges dismissed for lack of probable cause in the issuance of the search warrant. The validity of the search warrant would become a very much debated and crucial part of the case's outcome.

From the District Court Hearing, Judge Noah Rosenbloom presiding:

The Court: Good afternoon, ladies and gentlemen. The record may show it's now approximately 4:35; Defendant is here with Mr. Schade appearing in his behalf.

The Court: If you will see that he has a copy of the charging portion of the document in his hand, and if you will read the relevant portion into the record please, Mr. O'Connor.

Mr. O'Connor: (edited summary) Yes, Your Honor, The Complaint states that the following facts establish probable cause. The facts constitute the Complainant's basis for believing that the Defendant, on the 27th day of March, 1978, at 10 North Minnesota Street, New Ulm, Minnesota committed the following described offense: Retains possession of movable property of another, maximum sentence being 10 years or $10,000.00 fine or both. The Complaint is signed by Douglas Wiesner as the Complainant.

The Court: Mr. Meine, you have heard the Complaint read, and I believe you had a chance to read the copy yourself, is that true?

Mr. Meine: *Yes.*

The Court: And is it clear in your mind, sir, what the State claims you have done?

Mr. Meine: *Yes.*

The Court: And have you had a chance to review this matter with Mr. Schade as your counsel so he knows your side of it?

Mr. Meine: *Yes.*

The Court: And I assume he's explained to you there are various legal choices and options open to you at this time?

Mr. Meine: *Yes.*

The Court: Mr. Schade, is a further response appropriate at this time?

Mr. Schade: No, Your Honor.

The Court: Alright. Mr. O'Connor, are you able to tell me whether, if this case is tried, you will have evidence obtained in a search and seizure, in the nature of an admission or confession or obtained as a result of any of these?

Mr. O'Connor: Yes, Your Honor, and pursuant to rule 7.01 of the Rules of Criminal Procedure, served such a notice on Roger Hippert, whom I thought was representing him at this time of service.

Mr. Schade: We have the contents of Mr. Hippert's file, Your Honor, and we have a copy of the notice.

Mr. O'Connor: Basically what we claim pursuant to that Rule, Your Honor, is we have evidence seized pursuant to a search warrant; that in addition to that, we have confessions, admissions or statements in the nature of confessions made by the Defendant to various members of the New Ulm Police Department.

The Court: Have Counsel exchanged copies of these statements, whatever they are?

Mr. O'Connor: We have not exchanged copies of the statements because they were verbal, Your Honor.

The Court: So, you are able to tell Mr. Schade something about the circumstances, the surrounding circumstances, into which they were given so he has some way to identify what we are talking about?

Mr. O'Connor: I suppose if he were to ask I would respond to that question.

The Court: Well, I assume that you gentlemen will have an opportunity to exchange and explore that information in the next several days or whenever.

Mr. Schade: If I might suggest, Your Honor, we'd be requesting a Probable Cause Hearing and Omnibus Hearing, and I assume all of that information will be presented to the court at that time. I'm sure Mr. O'Connor will make it available to me prior to that time, but we would be asking the Court to schedule a date for an Omnibus Hearing and Probable Cause Hearing.

The Court: Do you feel you are in a position yet to make a motion to dismiss for lack of probable cause?

Mr. Schade: Well. I'm confident, Your Honor, I'll make a motion to dismiss for lack of probable cause and whether or not I do anything further depends upon what develops at the Omnibus Hearing.

The Court: I don't think that's quite the way its contemplated it would work, Mr. Schade, and you are satisfied that you are in a position to draw a conclusion on lack of probable cause at this point?

Mr. Schade: Well, the probable cause that I'm talking about primarily, Your Honor, would be the probable cause for the issuance of a search warrant.

The Court: Okay. So you're moving to suppress the results of the search, basically?

Mr. Schade: Correct.

The Court: Alright, fine. How long will it take to examine that?

(Then the judge and two attorneys discussed how much time would be needed for the next court appearance. They agreed on meeting again 2 p.m. on the 17th for up to an hour and a half.)

The Court: What's the situation as to bond here?

Mr. Schade: You're asking me, Your Honor?

The Court: I see there is a personal recognizance on file in the penal amount of $2,000.00. Is the state satisfied with that?

Mr. O'Connor: It is, Your Honor.

The Court: Mr. Meine, I routinely tell defendants at this point that the—to remind you that the recognizance includes the requirement that you keep the peace and be of good behavior, and I have no reason to believe you won't, but if something would come up, I don't want it to be a surprise to you that I would regard that as a violation of your bond.

Mr. Meine: *Thank You.*

As I left the courtroom in a hurry to return to my clothing store, I had mixed feelings about the way the hearings had begun. I was surprised to discover that Fred had changed lawyers from Al Mueller, Everett Young and Roger Hippert to Bill Schade, whom I knew very well. No plea was entered and Meine was released on his personal recognizance until his next appearance.

Meine's attorney was requesting a Probable Cause Hearing and Omnibus Hearing telling the court he planned on making a motion to dismiss the case for lack of probable cause—that being the issuance of, in his opinion, a defective search warrant. This action was being done in an attempt to suppress the results of the search warrant, and without that evidence, it would put our case in jeopardy.

As I left to go downtown, I pondered about all the things we had gone through in order to get the search warrant, and now there's a chance it might be ineffective in convicting Meine of this crime. How could this be possible? My chance of getting my inventory back, and my chance to save my business, might hang in the balance of the validity of the search warrant. What I'd heard in court did not make me happy, but Wm. T. O'Connor seemed very confident that the State had all they needed to "make their case" in less than fifteen minutes. At this point, I knew this would be a serious legal battle with the cunning Bill Schade versus the Brown County Attorneys. While round one was over, the court battle would continue.

The intensity of the situation was hitting an all-time high. I was trying to stay focused and not lose my perspective on what I must do to make the best of out a bad situation for our business and personal reasons. I immersed myself in my work, partly to keep my business affairs in order, and also to keep my mind off the legal issues of the pending trial.

At home, Konnie and I did our best to not let this disrupt our family life and things at school for our children. Our son, Christopher, at age eleven was the oldest of our children, and was very much aware what was happening. Today, when we talk about what happened back then, he tells me he remembers that I was upset and pacing in and out of church that Easter Sunday morning. He knew that something was terribly wrong. Children have such marvelous intuition, although as an adult he is still the same way.

The next hearing was scheduled for Monday, April 17. The New Ulm police officers that were most directly involved in the case testified as to the details of the case, especially the application for the search warrant and the issuance of the warrant. I read the police reports that were written by the officers upon completion of the search and seizure of the stolen inventory in Meine's store. The law enforcement investigation reports were filled with emotion from many perspectives.

New Ulm Policeman Warren Blomquist's report included the following selected comments:

On the evening of 3/26/78 Officer Wiesner called me at my home and advised me that he would like to have me at the station early on the morning of 3/27/78. He went on to explain briefly regarding the information available to this time relative to merchandise disappearing from the Leuthold Jensen Clothing Store.

After obtaining the search warrant Sgt. Schapekahm, Officer Wiesner and I then spent some time in the Jensen clothing store for the purpose of familiarizing ourselves with the merchandise we would be looking for. At approximately 2:00 P.M. Schapekahm, Wiesner, and myself then entered the Meine store where we found Fred Meine sitting on a table next to his cash register. Officer Wiesner explained our reason for being there and duly advised Mr. Meine of his rights. Mr. Meine indicated that he understood his rights, and after reading the Miranda form and waiver he signed same. Officer Wiesner then asked for Mr. Meine's cooperation in the matter and Meine answered by saying "do what you have to do."

We had been advised by the County Attorney to confiscate any items with missing labels. During this procedure Fred Meine remained in the store either in a chair near the middle of the store or a chair at the rear of the store. As the search continued through Monday, Tuesday, and Wednesday, Fred appeared to be following his normal routine as he went home for meals at the regular times and even performed some duties in the store. During a couple interludes I had the opportunity to talk with Mr. Meine, and both times he broke down and cried and expressed concern for his family. At one time on Wednesday he asked me, "Warren, do you know how many people have called me since this began? I responded by saying probably none, and he responded by saying I was right and then broke down again sobbing. When he regained his composure, he revealed that this lack of concern was no surprise to him as no one had offered to help him when his building burned a few years ago.

End of excerpts from Blomquist's investigation report

Chapter 22
Police Testify

By *The Journal*:

New Ulm Police officer Douglas Wiesner and Sergeant Charles Raabe testified Monday at a hearing in the case of the State of Minnesota vs. Fred Meine before Judge Noah Rosenbloom in Brown County District Court.

The officers related to the court their individual parts in obtaining the search warrant and the actual search and seizure conducted at Meine Clothing Company, 10 North Minnesota Street, New Ulm from March 27th to the 30th.

Meine's attorney, Bill Schade, questioned both police officers extensively about the details of the application and obtaining of the search warrant.

Referring to the constitutional rights concerning search and seizure, Schade filed a motion with the court to suppress evidence obtained during the search and seizure.

The lawyer said that the search warrant was "facially defective" for several reasons. Schade listed the use of hearsay, circumstantial evidence, and that the application for the warrant was signed "apparently not under oath."

Schade emphasized that on the search warrant there was "no description of the place to be searched" and concluded that the

"fruits of the search as well as statements cannot be used against Mr. Meine."

Judge Rosenbloom commented that he was not concerned with the circumstances surrounding the application for the search warrant, but that he did have some questions concerning the search warrant itself.

Rosenbloon decided to receive briefs from both lawyers before making any ruling.

Following the first hearing, a hearing in the case of Leuthold Jensen vs. Fred Meine was conducted. The judge ordered Charles Wilson, attorney for Leuthold Jensen, to submit a court order that would release any clothing held as evidence that the State did not claim as needed for the prosecution within ten days of the signing of the order.

New Ulm city officials would then be permitted to release the clothing obtained during the search and seizure of the Meine Store to either Leuthold Jensen or Meine, whichever party claimed the particular articles.

The search and seizure was conducted at Meine's Store after New Ulm Police obtained information that clothing missing from Leuthold Jensen Clothiers, adjacent to Meine's Store, was possibly being sold by Meine.

During the hearing, I listened to William Schade, the defense attorney offer the motion on behalf of the Defendant, Fred Mreine Jr., to suppress all of the evidence, whether it was as a result of the search and seizure or any admissions that Fred Meine, Jr. may have made to the law enforcement officers. I was aware that the defense was trying to "grab any straw" to get the charges dismissed. After listening to the testimony, I was more and more concerned that the judge would rule the warrant invalid and cause huge problems for our case. The argument that the defense raised to try to convince the judge that the warrant was invalid was because the description of the premises to be searched was not complete or detailed enough, and that the officer that served the warrant may not have been under oath.

New Ulm Police Officer Doug Wiesener testified and explained the process of serving the search warrant. I thought Cpl. Wiesner did a great job of remaining calm, professional and steady as he was grilled by the defense. Sergeant Raabe did an outstanding job as well, and was not riled when the defense attorney challenged some of his actions during the search of the Meine Store. This must be a difficult part of the job of being a police officer—doing their job and then defending their actions in court.

Attorney Schade offered a long explanation of the statutes upon which law enforcement must operate in exercising a valid search warrant. He went into great detail to present his view of how to interpret these statutes.

I left the court room somewhat down; I totally understood the importance of constitutional rights of citizens, but not when used as a shield to protect someone who's already admitted their guilt. The admissions by Meine, along with the tremendous amount of evidence and his comments to law enforcement, were the obvious "elephants in the room."

The second hearing that took place pertained to the civil lawsuit that we filed against Meine. It was encouraging news. The judge instructed our attorneys to submit a court order that would release any inventory that the State would not need as evidence in the case to either Leuthold Jensen's or Meine Clothing; whoever could prove ownership. We would file the order and hopefully would have the merchandise returned to us by the City of New Ulm who had temporary possession of it.

Chapter 23
More Charges

nother criminal hearing was scheduled for April 27 that would bring additional counts against Fred Meine Jr. This would be in the form of an amended complaint. I was told that the State considered the need for more evidence due to the judges's ruling that the search warrant was defective. This additional evidence was reassuring to me as I felt this may help in winning the case and getting our inventory back.

At this point I have to compliment Brown County attorneys James Olson, Bill O'Connor and Clark Tuttle who worked tirelessly to overcome many obstacles to fight for justice in this strange case. I respect these professional gentlemen and the office of the Brown County Attorney and appreciate what they did in handling the Meine case.

The State submitted the amended complaint that contained four additional counts against Meine. Thankfully for us, those four additional counts against Fred Meine, Jr. were accepted by Judge Rosenbloom.

The counts all dealt with specific sales of clothing—a suit to Eldon Traulich, a suit to Bart Hayes, a leather jacket to Mrs. Jim Schroeck, and a suit to Terry Prange. These were the result of purchases made by New Ulm area citizens at Fred Meine's clothing store. These people stepped forward in response to the County Attorney's appeal to the public, requesting anyone who had purchased an item of clothing from Meine's which had labels removed from it to notify their office. The three individuals mentioned above (Hayes, Prange and Schroeck) brought their purchases into the County Attorney's office. Eldon had purchased the suit from Meine as discussed earlier. It shows they were people of character, and their actions were a great help in the effort to bring Meine to justice.

The next attempt at getting the case against Meine dismissed by the attorneys for the Defendant was the filing of a petition to appeal to the Minnesota Supreme Court. After considerable deliberation Judge Rosenbloom denied the petition to appeal.

As the court hearings continued on over the next several months, I struggled to keep a positive focus. It was difficult to balance my life at home; keep my business from failing, stay involved with the legal process, and attend the court hearings.

Working on special events and community projects gave me a lift. I was a very active member of the New Ulm Chamber of Commerce. One of their showcase events was the annual Chamber Frolics—our annual business meeting, plus a variety show and dinner/dance that followed. One of those events is most memorable. The concept we chose was to mimic the popular country music television show "Hee Haw," hosted by singers Buck Owens and Roy Clark. It turned out great, was a sell-out and huge success. I co-hosted, along with Bob Ranweiler. Wearing gaudy tuxedos, we did a "stand up" comedy routine that we wrote with the help of our wives, Konnie and Gayle, and Mark Firle and his wife, Pam. We had so much fun writing the script at the Firles' home that we were in tears from laughing at our own jokes. Canned applause on a sound track was added to our silly skits and bits. Mark doing the Korn County News was hilarious. Many other Chamber members did a fantastic job as part of the cast of characters. So much fun! These events were super in helping the Chamber members get acquainted and work together in harmony, ultimately benefiting the entire community in building a strong business base. It gave me some needed comedy relief from the stress of my difficult business pressures. It always pays to be involved in your community and the Chamber, in particular.

The next hearing would be on Tuesday, May 16. I received a subpoena from the court to appear before the judge of the District Court for the Fifth Judicial District. While I was somewhat apprehensive, I was not too concerned about taking the stand. I would remind myself to take my time, tell the truth, and answer the questions to the best of my ability. This would end up being a long day in court.

The following is a news story from *The Journal:*

Dropping a piece of chewing gum in a public trash receptacle led to the discovery of the leak of his missing clothing, retail merchant Jim Jensen testified at a hearing today in Brown County District Court.

"When I pushed the lid," said Jensen, owner of the Leuthold Jensen Clothing Store, 14 North Minnesota Street, "I saw good coat hangers, and then I saw labels of clothing from my store. Such items are usually not junked, so I looked a little deeper and found letterheads from the Meine Clothing Store."

Jensen, called to the witness stand by the prosecution, said he had previously seen clothing in the Meine window that looked like his.

He contacted police who started action that led to Fred Meine,

proprietor of Meine Clothing, 10 North Minnesota Street, being charged
with possession of stolen property plus four counts of selling stolen
property.
  "Cpl. Douglas Wiesner of the New Ulm Police Department came to my
store at 5:30 P.M. Saturday, March 25, and we checked for a point of
entry other than the public doors," said Jensen. "There were cobwebs
over the windows in the basement under our original store, indicating
these were not the openings used. Then we came to a common door
between my store and Meine. I had not been suspicious of this (door)
since the hinges were on my side and also a hasp. But a close
investigation with a flashlight showed that a panel in the door in the
lower quarter had been sawed through. We could see gold colored
hinges on the other side."
  "On the header of the door, there were holes that had once been bored
for pipes or wire. We shined the flashlight through and recognized some
distinctive-colored shirts hanging in his basement."
  Jensen told his story at a continuation of the Meine Omnibus Hearing.
  On March 27, 1978, Jensen testified, Eldon Traulich was asked to buy
a suit in the Meine store.
  "I recognized it as my property," said Jensen, "and we got a search
warrant."
  Also testifying before Judge Noah Rosenbloom was judicial officer Pat
Moriarty, who told of examining the search warrant on March 27 while
waiting to have lunch at the Kaiserhoff restaurant. It was brought to him
by Wiesner.
  Robert Halvorson, an attorney, testified that he received a call the
evening of March 27 from Jensen asking him to represent the store. He
told of a meeting held 1:30 P.M., March 29 in the law offices of Al
Mueller, attorney for Meine at that time. Present, he said, were Meine,
Mueller, Roger Hippert, Jensen and Halvorson.
  At that meeting, said Halvorson, Meine agreed to permit Jensen to
search his store to secure his clothing, and this was carried out.
  William Schade was now representing Meine. Judge Rosenbloom had
ruled the search warrant was invalid.

I was glad this part of the hearing was over. I had never been on a witness
stand before. I did the best I could, but it was very difficult, and I was glad to
have given my testimony and be done with that for now.
  When Judge Rosenbloom stated he had ruled the search warrant invalid, I

was dissapointed, but not totally surprised. The judge's ruling was significant in the criminal case against Meine; a valid search warrant and the evidence was what we needed to get a conviction. All the work and hours of locating and inventorying the stolen clothing was suddenly in jepordy. The very thought of the possibility of losing the evidence was not good.

I was concerned about regaining possession of the clothing that belonged to us that was held as evidence. I was also concerned that Meine's attorney might get the case dismissed due to the lack of sufficient evidence.

It was disheartening to think that after all the years of our struggle to keep our business from failing, the loss of years of personal income, and the mental anguish, this case could come down to a technicality in regard to the search warrant. It almost seemed ridiculous to think that after discovering the mountain of evidence, this issue could potentially derail the case.

Now we would have to wait and see what would happen to our clothing that was locked up in the former post office building. Getting possession of my stolen goods would depend on the judge's ruling. I was anxious to get my inventory back because my stack of invoices was getting deeper; they needed to be paid. The other issue was that most of the people in our market had stopped buying men's clothing, anticipating a big stolen-merchandise recovery sale with drastic savings. The circumstances were getting very serious, and my vendors and creditors were not willing to keep waiting for their money. All the attention of the criminal case and the distractions from our day-to-day business caused our revenues to suffer. I was becoming desperate.

"When someone with money meets someone with experience, the person with the experience winds up with the money, and the person with the money winds up with the experience."

— *Harvey Mackay*

Chapter 24
Merchandise is Returned

Finally some good news. In the civil lawsuit, the Court ruled the inventory stored at the old post office building was legally our property. After receiving permission to take possession, we began the process of retrieving our stolen merchandise. This was no small task. It took the whole day and late into the evening, putting clothing on rolling racks, loading it in our cars, or carrying it over our shoulder to bring it back to our store on Minnesota Street. It was quite a parade of merchandise going down the alley next to the B&L Bar and across Minnesota Street. We stopped the traffic many times during the trek. I was relieved and thankful to be getting it back so we could raise some cash and pay our bills.

Steve Jacobson had been promoted to manage the Leuthold store in Albert Lea, Minnesota. He had done an outstanding job as my assistant manager, and I was happy that he would have an opportunity to manage and be a partner with the Leuthold Company. The timing wasn't the best with all the turmoil at our store, but we were glad Steve and Gay could have their own store.

As they say, "one door closes and another door opens." So true; I hired Scott Horner, another fine young gentleman who was a New Ulm native. He'd be my assistant manager. Scott was with me as we held the "theft-recovery sale," and the auction to dispose of the Meine fixtures and equipment. Scott did a very nice job working with me and was excellent in sales and customer service. Because of his track record at our store, Scott and his wife Marcia later had the chance to move on to manage their own store at Waterville, Minnesota.

The whole process of retrieving our clothing was a mammoth task, so I engaged the help of our friends. Once we had everything back in our store and cleaned and pressed all the items, we put on sale price tags, and placed them on racks by category. The recovered inventory was stored in the store's basements. We had to make room and get our store back to normal. After several days of planning and organization, we were about to begin the biggest sale, in terms of total dollars, in my retail career.

My main concern was that some of the inventory was nearly three years old and may be losing some its value and appeal. For this reason, as well as to capture the momentum of the public interest and curiosity in this very unusual event, we felt it was urgent to hold the sale as soon as possible. This would be the much-debated "GIANT THEFT-RECOVERY SALE."

With the court ruling giving us possession of the stolen merchandise, we assumed that it was fine to go ahead and have the sale, and that it would not affect the outcome of the pending criminal trial. Later on, this would be questioned by Mr. Meine's attorney as publicizing what we knew to be true.

The sale would be huge. People were begging us to sell them many of the items that we had tucked away in our basement, knowing they were going to get the "deal of a lifetime." They wanted to get a jump on the upcoming big sale.

After several weeks of preparation and planning, we released our advertising campaign on radio, television and newspapers. The sale was a fantastic success with eager buyers coming from all over the area to take advantage of our selection, quality and prices. The first day of the sale, the downtown area was jammed with cars and people, end to end. By the time the sale had ended, we had sold out almost everything, almost to the last button. The sale ran from June 9-19.

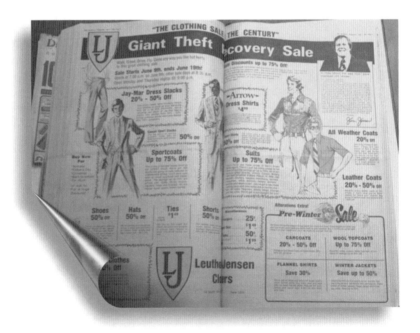

"The Clothing Sale of the Century," theft recovery sale

This was one of the few bright spots of the whole ordeal. Hopefully now we could get caught up on the bills and get back to the business of operating our men's clothing store without all the distractions. All that was left was waiting for the legal process to unfold as Fred Meine, Jr. would have to face the consequences of his devious

Stolen garments return to rack for 'alleged-theft recovery sale

By Linda Picone
Staff Writer

A good businessman knows how to turn adversity to his advantage.

So Jack Jensen decided to let a theft help his business, after about four years of hurting it.

Jensen declared an "alleged-theft recovery sale" at his New Ulm, Minn., store, Leuthold-Jensen Clothiers. It was an unusual reason for a sale, but then the theft had been unusual as well.

Shortly after his store expanded in 1975, Jensen began missing certain pieces of men's clothing. He ran a security check and had the locks changed a year later, but the thefts continued.

This past March, Jensen spotted a customer wearing a suit that looked like one missing from his store. The suit had no labels, but the customer said he bought it at the clothing store next door.

Fred J. Meine Jr., the owner of that store, was arrested and charged with possessing and transferring movable property of another. Police

allege that Meine had been taking clothing from the two stores. Meine has not been tried yet.

During their investigation, police officers seized the stolen clothing and inventoried it. Only a few pieces were needed for the trial, so the rest was returned to Jensen and Jensen decided to add some clothing from his regular stock and give a sale.

The "alleged-theft recovery sale" started Friday and goes through next Monday. For at least the first two days, the store was packed elbow-to-elbow, according to Steve Jacobson, assistant manager.

Although merchandise had been disappearing since 1975, Jacobson said most of the recovered merchandise is "very current." The thief, he said, had been "progressively more selfish" and had taken more items recently than in the early years.

Jacobson thinks that one reason the sale has done so well — besides the discounts — was the news coverage of the theft. "The publicity we've had is pretty good," he said. "It's a lot of free advertising."

This story appeared in a Twin Cities newspaper where they identified me as "Jack" Jensen

actions as the "next-door neighbor and thief."

I guess we created quite "an up-roar" with our Theft-Recovery Sale. My attorney said that Meine's attorney was livid that we held the sale before the pending criminal trial had begun. I really saw no harm in what we had done because Fred had admitted to the police that he had taken my inventory, and had sold some of it. Fred had also given up any claim to the merchandise that was being held in the post office building.

Attorney Bill Schade would now make an attempt to get the trial moved out of Brown County, as he felt Fred would not receive a fair trial due to the news stories, our sale ads and the general feeling of how the area people perceived what Fred Meine Jr. had done.

Many media people were brought in to testify as to the wording of the advertisements, the number of times the ads ran, and to the number of people their media source reached. Some of the media representatives who testified included John Husack of KEYC TV, Perry Galvin of KNUJ radio, plus, Steven Fox and Steve Grosam of The Journal. They all gave similar testimony in regard to what had appeared on their media outlets.

Chapter 25
A Change of Venue

Excerpts from *The Journal*:

Because of pretrial publicity, particularly, a newspaper advertisement, the trial of Fred Meine, Jr. will be held in Lyon County rather than Brown County.

Judge Noah Rosenbloom informed Meine's attorneys Thursday that their motion for a change of venue will be granted. The trial, which may be held in September at the earliest, will be heard by District Court Judge Miles Zimmerman.

Originally, one of Meine's attorneys, William Schade requested the trial be moved to Duluth because of newspaper accounts of Meine's arrest in March for the sale and possession of stolen property.

Schade's main objection to the publicity, both in print and on television, was an advertisement for a "Giant Theft Recovery" sale.

The advertisement stated, among other things, that the case has been solved and most of what you've heard or read is probably true.

The sale was held after clothing store merchant Jim Jensen recovered a large amount of items stolen over a four year period. Estimates put the loss over that period at more than $100,000.

The clothing was recovered from the store of his next-door neighbor and long time competitor, Fred Meine, whom police served with a search warrant after a decoy buy was set up.

Evidence obtained in that search, however, was ruled

inadmissible in court because the county attorney's office drew up the warrant improperly.

As a result, the county attorney's office filed new charges against Meine based on clothing that was allegedly taken from Leuthold Jensen but purchased, allegedly, by four individuals at Meine's.

The motion for a change of venue was protested Monday by James Olson, an assistant county attorney. Olson said anyone affected by the media coverage would be screened out in the jury-selection process. He also said moving the trial would be an unnecessary expense to the county.

The expense would be lessend somewhat, however, since Judge Rosenbloom moved the trial to Lyon County instead of St. Louis County.

Judge Rosenbloom will not be hearing the case because of an affidavit of prejudice filed against him by Schade. Every attorney has the right to file such an affidavit.

Since his arrest, Meine has closed his clothing store and moved to the Twin Cities, where hs is now working.

Chapter 26
Guilty Plea

I had been told that there had been serious discussions about Fred entering a plea of guilty in order to avoid a long, difficult and embarrassing court trial. The trial had been officially transferred to Lyon County by an order of change of venue and assigned to Judge Miles Zimmerman. However, before the trial would begin, Fred Meine pled guilty.

The phone rang when I was at home having dinner with my family. It was the news that Fred would be pleading

Meine pleads guilty to thefts

guilty to the crime of possessing and selling my stolen merchandise. Hanging up, I sighed with relief that it would soon be over and done. One year of concern since we discovered the secret of our mystery, but the court hearings and turmoil felt more like ten years. Happy to get the news, the end of the marathon was in sight.

I was present at the Blue Earth County Courthouse in Mankato when Fred Meine entered his plea of guilty. It was a very moving and emotional experience for me as I listened to the questioning of Fred Meine, Jr., and his responses. The trial was scheduled to start March 20, 1979 almost a year from the date we discovered the black plastic suit hangers. With the trial by jury about to begin, it appeared the attorneys for Meine realized the case would be difficult to win, and chose to recommend to their client to enter the guilty plea.

Included are selected portions of the very interesting transcript extracted from my research at the Brown County

Courthouse, which tells of Fred Meine, Jr. entering his plea of guilty. I will let you read what Fred had to say.

The matter came duly for Hearing before the Honorable Judge Miles B. Zimmerman on the 9th day of March, 1979, at 9:00 a.m., at Mankato, Minnesota. Mr. James R. Olson appeared on behalf of the State of Minnesota and Mr. William M. Schade, attorney, appeared for the Defendant.

The Court: I had set the hearing today on any further motions that Counsel may want to make prior to the start of the trial which I have scheduled for March 20th, and as I understand it now, there have been some plea negotiations.

Mr. Olson: That is correct, Your Honor. Since the last time we were in court, which was about two or three weeks ago, I have been in contact with Mr. Schade on behalf of Mr. Meine, and Mr. Schade has indicated to me that after consulting with his client, his client is willing to enter a plea of guilty to Count II of the Amended Complaint. Your honor, I have given this some thought, and I feel a plea to Count II is justified, and the agreement would be that if the Court accepts the plea to Count II of the Complaint that we would then dismiss Counts I, III, IV and V.

The Court: All right, Mr. Meine, would you come up here please? Stand over there so the Reporter can hear you. How old are you?

The Defendant: *59.*

The Court: What's your birth date?

The Defendant: *February 24, 1920.*

Q. Where do you live at the present time?

A. *83 West Arlington, Apartment 109.*

Q. Maybe you had better turn so the reporter can hear you. Face me.

A. *Alright, 83 West Arlington, Apartment 109, St. Paul, Minnesota.*

Q. Now, you have heard, have you not, Mr. Olson's statement that the State would agree to dismiss Counts I, III, IV and V if you pled guilty to Count II. The State would not make any recommendation as to what the sentence would be and leave it up to the Court. Do you understand that?

A. *Yes, sir.*

Q. You understand that what the Court does here is up to the Court?

A. *Yes.*

Q. Do you think this is what you want to do?

A. *Yes, sir.*

The Court: All right, then to Count II which charge you with wrongfully, unlawfully, feloniously, and intentionally and without claim of right that you did transfer the possession of movable property of another without his consent with the intent to deprive the owner permanently of possession of said property. To wit: a Johnny Carson tan, 44 extra-long suit, with vest and slacks too, that you transferred this by sale presumably to one, Eldon Traulich, of New Ulm. The suit being worth in excess of $100.00. Do you understand that this is the charge I'm asking you to plead to?

The Defendant: *I do.*

The Court: How do you plead to that charge?

The Defendant: *Guilty.*

The Court: All right, before I accept that plea Mr. Meine, I have to be satisfied that you do this voluntarily, knowingly with full understanding of what the consequences of your plea might be. I want to be sure that you understand in pleading guilty, you give up certain rights which any defendant has who is charged with a crime. I want to inquire into the background of this offense to make sure that the facts support the charge, and lastly, I want to inquire into your past and present record to assist me in making disposition of this matter. I'm therefore going to ask that you go over there and be sworn, and then we'll ask you some questions under oath.

The Court: You understand, Mr. Meine, what the purpose of this questioning is now?

The Defendant: *I do.*

The Court: Do you have any questions?

The Defendant: *No.*

The Court: Do you want a minute or two to compose yourself?

The Defendant: *Go ahead.*

The Court: Do you want some water?

The Defendant: *No, thank you.*

The Court: The Count to which you have pled guilty, charges you basically with having taken one suit from Leuthold Jensen Clothiers and sold this suit to—who was that again?

Mr. Olson: Eldon Traulich, Your Honor.

The Court: Traulich. You understand that that is the charge?

The Defendant: *I understand that.*

Q. Did you in fact do that?

A. *I did.*

Q. When did this occur, do you know?

A. *Monday, March 27, 1978. Yes, sir.*

Q. Do you recall that specifically, that specific instance?

A. *I do.*

Q. You understand also that the other charges or four charges, charge you with taking—Count I, for instance a large number of slacks, suits, shirts, leather jackets, and neckties, you understand that?

A. *I do.*

Q. Was this suit taken in connection with any of these? Let me put it to you this way, how many times did you make entry into Leuthold Jensen's?

A. *I do not recollect. I do not know, sir.*

Q. More than once?

A. *Quite a few times, yes.*

Q. Does your statement cover this?

A. *Yes, it does.*

Q. For the record then, Exhibit A indicates that a man came to your store—who was this? Would this be—?

A. *Eldon Traulich.*

Q. And I'm going to sort of summarize this, and asked to see a size 44 extra-long polyester suit of clothes and that he had been fitted on a previous occasion. You put the coat on him and he said he would take it, and that he would take it without alterations, which struck you as rather strange, because you had just taken that suit from Leuthold Jensen's, is that right?

A. *Correct.*

Q. You had entered the store through a panel in a common basement door, is that correct?

A. *Correct.*

Q. You state that you had slithered through this narrow opening in the early morning and had removed the Leuthold label from the garment before hanging it in stock. In a short while, the authorities were in your store with a search warrant, is that correct?

A. *That's correct.*

Q. That would be March 27th?

A. *1978.*

Q. You had taken this a few days before, right?

A. *Correct.*

Q. All right, we'll just take a moment here while I glance through this. The store that you operate, what was the name of that?

A. *Fred Meine Clothing Company.*

Q. Did you own that business?

A. *Well, it was incorporated.*

Q. You were the sole stockholder?

A. *No, I was not.*

Q. Who else?

A. *Well, my sister also.*

Q. She's not involved in this, is she?

A. *No, she has no involvement whatsoever.*

Q. No knowledge of it?

A. *No knowledge, no involvement, period.*

Q. Did she work with you in the business?

A. *No, she did not help me, no.*

Q. So she didn't know what was going on?

A. *No, nobody knew.*

Q. Until it broke out, she had no knowledge?

A. *Correct, nobody had any knowledge whatsoever.*

Q. All right, does the corporation own the business?

A. *It did, yes.*

Q. And the building?

A. *No, we were tenants.*

Q. Who owned the building?

A. *Henry Somsen.*

Q. And you rented it from him?

A. *Yes, sir.*

Q. Was this a single-story building or two-story?

A. *Actually, I would say it's a three story building.*

Q. What's above it?

A. *Well, it's rented out to various tenants.*

Q. Apartments or businesses?

Q. *Yes, it's apartments.*

Q. When did you first discover that there was some way of getting into the adjoining building, or did you make an opening?

A. *I just made an opening.*

Q. How did you do that?

A. *With an electric saw.*

Q. Through stone, wood or what?

A. *Through the panel of the common door.*

Q. Had there been a common door there? Was this a common wall?

A. *There always had been a common door there between us. In fact, we had a ....right down the stairs, when we went right down stairs in our store, there was a washroom, and formerly before Leuthold—and Leuthold Jensen had moved in next door, they'd use that common washroom, and later on, the door was closed between the two stores.*

Q. When was that done?

A. *To the best of my recollection, it would be when Jim Jensen became the proprietor of the Leuthold Jensen Clothing Store.*

Q. Who owns that building, do you know?

A. *Also, Henry Somsen.*

Q. How long have you been in business at that location?

A. *Since 1908 my father had been in business.*

Q. How were you doing financially?

A. *Then?*

Q. Then, about the time this broke out?

A. *Not too well.*

Q. What led you to start something like this?

A. *Lack of finances.*
Q. Were you making a living off this business?
A. *Barely.*
Q. Do you have children?
A. *I have two children.*
Q. Grown?
A. *Grownup, yes, 26 and 29.*
Q. Is your wife employed?
A. *She wasn't at the time. She is today.*
Q. Am I right in assuming that the first knowledge your family had of this was when this broke?
A. *That's correct.*
Q. Over how long a period of time was it that you were taking stuff from Jensen's?
A. *Approximately two and a half years.*
Q. What led you to conceive that idea?
A. *Financially, I was in dire straits. I cannot put the exact moment.*
Q. Do you handle the same brands of clothing?
A. Some of them.
Q. Incidentally, is this your handwriting, these statement?
A. *It is.*
Q. Do you commonly print?
A. *Invariably I do because I was taught that when I worked with the State Employment Service. I was taught how to print properly, hopefully.*
Q. But at all the times you were doing this, when you started, and go up to and including the time that you took the coat—the suit with which you are charged here, you knew you had no right to do so?
A. *I knew that.*
Q. And you took it with the intention of keeping it, selling it?
A. *Correct.*
Q. It would represent a 100% profit for you, wouldn't it?
A. *Correct.*
Q. Did you sell the clothes at less than what you regarded as market value?
A. *I did not.*
Q. How much of this stuff did you take?
A. *I have no idea.*
Q. Has there been an inventory made?
A. *I never inventory that type of merchandise.*
Q. Did you sell all of it?
A. *No, I surely didn't.*
Q. How much of it did you sell?
A. *I assume and I'm not very positive, perhaps $15,000.*

Q. How much did you take?

A. *I have no idea.*

Q. You say $15,000, are you talking about retail value?

A. *I'm talking about retail value.*

Q. Well, you must have some idea, how often did you go in there? When you went in there what would you take. How much? Would you be selective in what you took?

A. *Very selective, yes.*

Q. Pardon.

A. *Very selective.*

Q. You were acquainted with the interior of their store?

A. *Yes, very well.*

Q. I assume you went in there at night or was it weekends?

A. *Generally early in the morning.*

Q. What time?

A. *Six a.m., perhaps, something like that.*

Q. What would you do with the merchandise that you took?

A. *Well, I'd take it through their store, down the basement steps and put it through that panel in the door and take it back up the stairs and cut out the labels, put it in stock.*

Q. Cut the labels on what? Everything?

A. *Well, no, just cut off the Leuthold Jensen labels.*

Q. What type of suits did he handle? Johnny Carson?

A. *Yes, he had some Penn State, he ...*

Q. Were these the same brands that you handled?

A. *I handled Penn State.*

Q. How about Johnny Carson?

A. *No, we did not handle that.*

Q. You stole and sold Johnny Carson?

A. *That's correct.*

Q. That's the one you sold to Traulich?

A. *Correct.*

Q. Did you think you were going to get caught?

A. *I'm not sure.*

Q. Didn't you think about that?

A. *Many times.*

Q. Did you ever attempt to unburden yourself to someone about this?

A. *I was afraid to.*

Q. What's your educational background, Mr. Meine?

A. *I have a major in psychology and one in sociology from the College of St. Thomas in St. Paul.*

Q. Did you graduate?

A. *Yes.*

Q. What year?

A. *1942.*

Q. You didn't do this out of any motive other than the fact you were in financial straits?

A. *No.*

Q. What was your income annually when you started doing this?

A. *Oh, my income perhaps was around $8,000 per year.*

Q. Were you living on that?

A. *Yes, we were.*

Q. Sending kids to school?

A. *Yes.*

Q. Did you have a savings?

A. *Very small. Fortunately our daughter went to Mankato State to the University. She was very, very thrifty and she had been working through college. Our son had been in the Air Force for four years. He is extremely thrifty. He has his own little business as a sideline. He has been very—financially successful in that.*

Q. How old are your children?

A. *26 and 29.*

Q. Are they both married?

A. *Neither one is married. My daughter is employed by North Central Airlines. Our son is completing his fourth year at Gustavus Adolphus College in St. Peter. He's desirous of being a CPA. He has worked for the Federal Deposit Insurance Corporation.*

Q. Have you—when you got out of college, what did you do? Did you work for your dad?

A. *Actually, no. When I graduated from college it was wartime, and my father looked at me and he says, "Fred, look for your own job. I do not have any work for you." For a moment*

Q. Just tell me what have you done, what kind of work?

A. *Well, then I talked my way into a job in the Accounting Department for the E.I. DuPont—*

Q. How long did you work there?

A. *Six months until I was finally drafted. I was finally drafted by the U.S. Army when I was no longer considered blind, and I received a disabling injury during World War II.*

Q. Where was that? What happened?

A. *Well, I suffered a—fracture of left radius and left humerus.*

Q. From an automobile accident?

A. *No, I just slipped and fell*

Q. Is that why you use a cane now?

A. *No, this is from my phlebitis, I have poor blood circulation.*

Q. What is the state of your health, do you have some health problems?

A. *Yes, I certainly do.*

Q. What?

A. *As I stated, I have blood circulation problems. In fact, way back in April after getting out of bed—*

Q. I'm going to have you examined, but just tell me, what you have besides phlebitis?

A. *My blood circulation is very poor.*

Q. Do you have a heart condition?

A. *No.*

Q. Have you ever been hospitalized for any reason other than the fracture?

A. *No.*

Q. How long have you carried the cane?

A. *Since November 24, 1971, when I suffered my phlebitis attack.*

Q. I thought you said something about blindness, are you having eye problems, too?

A. *Well, it was just that the law considered me blind at that time.*

Q. Why?

A. *Because anybody that had 20/100 vision was considered—*

Q. Essentially blind?

A. *Well, yes, for the military, and I had vision of 20 over 375 at that time.*

Q. Correctable with glasses?

A. *Correct, right.*

Q. What's the condition you have, do you know?

A. *Well, it's the same way; it's never improved and never will improve. In fact, it's actually worse.*

Q. Do you have any other health problems?

A. *Well, nothing actually. I just have a (pause) of my left elbow*

Q. How long have you been in that clothing store?

A. *Well, actually when I was a child I used to help my father out.*

Q. When did you take it over?

A. *My father passed away June 27th of 1950, and I had been on the road selling for Lever Brothers, and I resigned my position because I realized my father had a malignancy, terminal and he would be dying shortly.*

Q. Then you came back to New Ulm and took over the business?

A. *Correct.*

Q. Do you own your own home?

A. *Yes, it's fully paid, yes, sir.*

Q. What is the value of your home? Do you still own it?

A. *Yes, I certainly do.*

Q. You're not living in it though, are you?

A. *No, there's nobody living there. Our son comes home generally speaking every weekend.*

Q. Do you propose to stay in the Cities?

A. *Yes, sir, I'm afraid I have to, yes.*

Q. Do you feel rejected as far as this community is concerned now?

A. *We realize that, yes.*

Q. Do you feel any sense of being persecuted on account of this or do you feel it's something you have coming?

A. *It's something I have coming, I realize it only too well.*

Q. Have you engaged in any community activities or welfare or activities that are helpful to others?

A. *As I stated in my confession, over a period of 25 years, I befriended many youngsters from broken families. In one case the father was an alcoholic and the mother had rejected her husband. Another one was—*

Q. Did you take the kids in to live with you?

A. *No, what I did was—the children would come into the store and would make some small purchase or would just talk, and while talking I realized they did have a problem at home, and therefore I gave them all the love and attention they required that they never received at home.*

Q. How could you explain an attitude of care in someone like that, and at the same time doing what you do?

A. *I cannot explain it.*

Q. Do you feel you are in debt to Mr. Jensen as the result of this still?

A. *Yes, in many ways I'm sure I'm in debt to Mr. Jensen.*

Q. Is there any way that you can think of that could work that out?

A. *I think it's all up to Mr. Jensen. If there is any way I can make things right, I would sure like to do it.*

Q. Morally, you recognize the sense of having to do this?

A. *I certainly do.*

Q. And to make restitution?

A. *I do.*

Q. Have you committed any other crime, Mr. Meine?

A. *None whatsoever.*

Q. Have you ever been arrested before?

A. *No, just for speeding. I have been investigated twice by the F.B.I.*

Q. For what?

A. *Well, for positions in the government.*

Q. Oh, you mean security checks?

A. *For DuPont, yes.*

Q. Where were you born?

A. *In New Ulm.*

Q. Have you discussed fully in these statements everything that you remember about these—first of all, the Traulich theft and secondly the thefts in general?

A. *To the best of my recollection, yes.*

Q. What do you think I ought to do with you?

A. *This is up to the Court to decide, not for myself to decide.*

Q. Have you ever been in jail?

A. *Never.*

Q. Have you ever visited a jail?

A. *Never.*

Q. What do you think your reaction would be to being in jail?

A. *We have discussed it many times in our home, both my wife and myself agreed to one thing. If I am—*

Q. Well, I don't want any further discussion on that subject.

The Court: Very well, the plea is accepted and may be entered. I'm not going to sentence you at this time. I'm going to ask that the Department of Corrections make a pre-sentence investigation. I'm going to ask that you submit to a medical examination and also a psychological examination by doctors that will have to be satisfactory to the Court. Hopefully, this can be done by April 9th, and we'll set sentencing for you for April 9th, at 2:30 in the afternoon.

The Court: Do you have any questions, Mr. Meine?

The Defendant: *None, whatsoever.*

The Court: Does Counsel have any questions?

Mr. Olson: The State has nothing further, Your Honor.

I walked out of the court room, very tired and more than ready to have all the publicity over with. I began my drive back home west on U.S. Highway 14 to New Ulm. I kept thinking back to the day we found the evidence that would blow open the case and help to discover who was stealing our inventory. I thought about the bizarre nature of what had happened, and how I would have to do my best to rebuild my business that had been going so well prior to Fred's plan to steal our merchandise. I wondered how these things can happen, and why us?

Looking back, I know I became a stronger person by having to reach deep inside myself to work my way through all of the issues that surrounded the whole incident. I also put extra effort into giving every customer the very best service possible. I always loved selling, and during these difficult days of my retail years, I worked extra hard at sales excellence. I believe this helped us stay in business. The more difficult our situation became, the harder we had to work at increasing our sales. Rolling down my car window, I breathed in some fresh air; things would be better now.

I, my family and my employees had just spent years of concern as to loss of profits due to the expense of buying merchandise, only to have it go unexplainably missing—and then a year of all the legal matters and extra expenses. You may find interesting *The Journal*'s following account of Fred's "anguish."

From *The Journal*:

"It all began, to the best of my knowledge, approximately 2 ½ years before the fatal Monday, March 27, 1978. I employed the use of an electric saw to cut my way through a panel of the wooden door leading from the basement of the Fred Meine Clothing Company...."

So begins the long, sometimes penitent, sometimes matter-of-fact confession of former New Ulm merchant Fred Meine, Jr. to theft and selling clothing belonging to his neighbor and main competitor, Jim Jensen of Leuthold Jensen Clothiers. The meticulously hand-printed testimonial addressed to "The Honorable District Judge Miles Zimmerman" describes, step by step, the events leading up to the commission of the crimes, the arrest, and aftermath.

Meine was arrested for selling a stolen suit to Eldon Traulich of New Ulm one year ago. But the suit was only one of many Meine slipped through an opening in an old wooden basement door separating his clothing store from his neighbors over a two-and-a-half-year period.

In his confession, Meine describes to the court how he laboriously cut a hole through a panel in an old wooden door dividing his store and Leuthold Jensen's, despite his unhealthy disposition and lack of mechanical ability. He tells how he then fastened screws to the top of the hewn panel and painted it a deep brown to camouflage it.

The commission of the crimes was not easy for Meine—they strained both his body and his mind. Because of his poor blood circulation, phlebitis and an old war injury to his forearm (he fell down). Meine had trouble *"slithering through"* the small space he had cut.

His handicaps also meant that he could only carry small amounts of clothing from the store next door. Each trip, which usually occurred on Sunday mornings *"when the main street New Ulm was serene,"* would take two to three hours.

But for Meine, Sundays were anything but serene.

"Through the many times that I entered into the basement of the Leuthold Jensen store, I had the dreadful fear of being apprehended. It made me nervous and irritable. Even though I did not sell a great amount of stolen merchandise, I was always apprehensive about this aspect."

Despite the difficulties, he must have made the trip many, many times—the stolen merchandise is estimated to be worth more than $100,000.

But why, the court asked Meine—the same questions his friends, his *family and he himself have been asking ever since that fatal day of his arrest. Meine told the judge he hatched the crime scheme out of desperation. His store was in dire straits financially, while his neighbor and arch business rival, Leuthold Jensen, prospered. He had no debts, but he said his income from the store amounted to little more than $8,000 per year—not a great deal of money to support a wife and two children through college.*

But why continue stealing when so little of the merchandise was put on the racks for sale? In fact, Meine sold only about 10% of the stock he stole or about $15,000 worth. Much of the merchandise he kept in his basement—so much in fact, he began to run out of hanging racks. He had no answer for the court.

Perhaps it was an obsession. Perhaps it was a spiteful jealousy of his prosperous neighbor, or an attempt to drive his main competitor out of business. Meine wouldn't say. Perhaps he doesn't know.

Meine described in detail for the court "the fatal day" a year ago when he sold a freshly stolen suit to a customer, Eldon Traulich. Jensen had asked Traulich to buy the suit, suspecting the suit was from his store because only he, not Meine, carried that line of clothing.

On the morning of March 27, 1978, a slender, high-strung man asked to see a size 44 extra-long solid tan polyester suit he had fitted the previous Saturday. I slipped the suit coat onto the gentleman's shoulders, and after quickly examining it while standing in front of the sway mirror, he stated that he would take it. Even though the garment required extensive alterations, he begged off this work. He stated that he was going on a trip to Africa in a few days. His extremely nervous condition left me apprehensive as this suit had just been stolen from my next-door neighbor, the Leuthold Jensen clothing store.

"As it turned out I was correct in assuming that something was amiss. The nervous customer was Eldon Traulich, who was sent in to cause my downfall."

Although law enforcement authorities found many other stolen suits in Meine's store, it was this single crime to which Meine tearfully pleaded guilty Friday morning in Blue Earth District Court before Judge Zimmerman. Although he nearly lost his composure when he took the stand, he refused a recess, telling the court to "go ahead." He had chosen to forgo the anguish and embarrassment of a long jury trial by confessing his crimes and surrendering his fate to the court. Four other similar counts were dismissed by the court in accepting Meine's plea—an arrangement agreeable to the prosecuting attorney James Olson and the defense attorney, William Schade.

But Meine's reprieve from further litigation cannot match the "untold mental anguish (suffered by) the Meine family." Compared to this anguish, the closing of the Fred Meine Clothing store after 70 years in business (Meine's father founded the store) was incidental. Even his family's increased financial hardship cannot compare to the shame and anguish they felt.

"My misdeed caused my wife to lose almost all her friends as they refused to associate with her. Our telephone seldom rang anymore, and the little social life that she had with her girlfriends ceased to exist. She has difficulty in sleeping at night because of the shame, and the continued publicity.

"Our children had their moments too as the national publicity took its toll. It was very obvious they were ashamed of what their father had done."

My sister withstood the pressure until just a few weeks ago when she finally decided to resign her position as secretary of the New Ulm Chamber of Commerce after 31 years of service. She has suffered from mental anguish for too many months."

Meine told how even "the many youngsters I had befriended during the past 25 years have not sought to visit me or wish us well. Over the years I have served many as a substitute father. Many had lost one of their parents or came from broken homes. I have always been available to assist them in making important decisions in their lives. All have become successful, for which I am grateful. Each and every one of them required proper direction, love, patience and understanding. I hope that I was instrumental in some way to their achieving what they have."

"The last 347 days have been a holocaust for my entire family. It has left the culprit, physically and emotionally drained. My present employment position (he sells clothes in St. Paul) is in severe jeopardy as is my wife's. Very few employers are compassionate, as well as forgiving. My life hangs on a single slender thread at this time. My compunction is overwhelming."

Meine's plight is not over with his admission to his crimes. He still faces sentencing which could cost him $5,000 and five years of his life. Judge Zimmerman said he doubted he would penalize Meine with a stiff jail sentence, partly because of Meine's ill health, partly because it wouldn't do any good.

His New Ulm house, which he has yet to give up, stands empty now. His store, after 70 years of business, is hardly recognizable, having been incorporated into Leuthold Jensen's. His son and daughter have left town, gone to start new lives elsewhere. He and his wife can never return to the town he grew up in.

When I read *The Journal*'s story of Fred's years of anguish, it was upsetting that Fred, who obviously ran the gamut of many emotions, both while in the act of stealing, and then from the resulting events after he was caught, never once seemed to feel—certainly never expressed any remorse or concern at the harm he may have caused us. He never apologized to me, my family or anyone from the Leuthold Company. He never verbally or in writing expressed any remorse for what he had done to us.

Some months later I would see Fred at the gas station or in the grocery store parking lot in New Ulm. On those occasions, he would make eye contact, and then look away. I feel he had several opportunities to say something to me in the way of an apology, but he never did.

Chapter 27
The Confession

The following is the text of a hand-written confession that Fred Meine, Jr. submitted to Judge Miles Zimmermann:

To: The Honorable Judge Miles Zimmermann

It all began, to the best of my knowledge, approximately two and a half years before the fatal Monday, March 27, 1978. I employed the use of an electric saw to cut my way through a panel of the wooden door leading from the basement of the Fred Meine Clothing Company of 10 North Minnesota Street, New Ulm, Minnesota to the basement of the Leuthold Jensen store of 14 North Minnesota Street. I fastened some screws to the top of the hewn panel in order that it would permit me to enter and exit through this panel whenever I deemed it necessary. I swept the sawdust and broken bits of wood from the floor in order that there would be no evidence of my entry into the Leuthold Jensen store basement. I fastened the top of the panel so that it was hinged and would swing up and towards the Leuthold basement when it was opened. I was able to enter the Leuthold Clothing store's basement through this narrow opening at my discretion. Generally I would crawl through this restricted opening on Sunday mornings when the main street of New Ulm was serene. I would, thereupon, select the merchandise very carefully from the Leuthold Clothing store racks and shelves. Due to the handicap of my left arm as well as my poor legs, I could only carry a limited amount of selected men's clothing and furnishings through the Leuthold Clothing Store, then down their basement steps, then through their basement to the small opening in the panel of the door leading to the Meine Clothing Store basement. After manipulating this stolen merchandise through the cut panel in this basement door, I would thereupon carry it up the Meine staircase to the main floor of the store, whereupon I would remove any Leuthold Jensen labels from all the items of clothing. Then I would

Continued...

hang the stolen merchandise onto the racks of the Meine Clothing Store. On each occasion that I would enter the Leuthold Store it would require from two to three hours of effort. I proceeded to paint the entire door in the basement of the Leuthold Jensen Clothing Store to a deep brown to keep the suspicion from the cut in the panel door. On the side of the cut panel of the door, I fastened a piece of Masonite with ordinary screws, which could be refastened when so desired. Since I possess a very limited amount of mechanical ability, I used my knowledge of physics and practiced cutting with a saw through a door panel located in the men's room in the Meine basement. Through such diligent experimentation, I was able to calculate the proper angle required in order that the cut panel could be hinged at the top when it would swing outward and up. Even though my woodwork was very crude, it did serve the intended purpose. Through the many times that I entered into the basement of the Leuthold Jensen Store, I had the dreadful fear of being apprehended. It made me nervous and irritable. Even though I did not sell a great amount of the stolen merchandise, I was always apprehensive about this aspect. Due to the quantity of stolen merchandise in the Meine Store basement, I was cautious about permitting anyone into that portion of the store. I did not have adequate hanging space as well as shelves for this merchandise. I wore very little of this stolen merchandise as I require made-to-measure clothing to properly fit my body. Invariably I would enter the Leuthold Jensen Clothing Store at an early hour on a Sunday morning. I was quite selective of the type of men's clothing that I would steal, and therefore I found it unprofitable on my occasions into their store as the quality of men's fashions has noticeably declined.

Fred Meine Jr.

During the hearings and after Fred pled guilty, to me, Fred's attitude about his crime appeared cold and detached. Although he confessed his guilt (in his own handwriting), he maintained an air of being "somewhat above" the whole process of being brought to justice. Some of his comments in his confession irritated me, in particular his jab about having to be selective in stealing my merchandise due to the noticeable decline in the quality of the clothing.

After Fred's confession of guilt, and after reaching a settlement in the civil lawsuit we had filed against him, the court awarded us possession of his remaining inventory, fixtures and equipment. We proceeded with a sale to dispose of the Meine clothing inventory. The next step was to have a public auction to sell the fixtures and equipment that were in Fred's store. The auction was held at the Meine Store on a Sunday afternoon. It went very well and drew a large crowd due to antique status of the fixtures and the publicity the story had

The interior of Fred's store before we began the remodeling

generated. We made arrangements to lease the Meine store location in order to increase our store size for future growth. We would began the process of remodeling; creating another new dimension to our business.

Waiting to hear what sentence Judge Zimmerman would pass on Fred Meine Jr. for crimes committed against us, I had mixed feelings about what I wanted the judge to do. Mostly I just wanted to get it over and done, and try to forget and forgive. Part of me wanted to see Meine go to jail, and part of me wanted him to be on probation and not serve a prison sentence. I was glad the decision was not mine to make.

The Court: Mr. Meine, would you come up here, please. On March 9th of this year, you entered a plea of guilty to Theft; that Count of the Complaint which charges you with the theft of a suit which was sold to one Eldon Traulich. Are you satisfied that you want your plea to that charge to stand?

The Defendant: *Yes, Your Honor.*

The Court: The Court will accept that plea, and the remaining counts of the Complaint which would be I, III, IV and V are dismissed. By virtue of this plea you stand convicted of this offense, and it is my obligation to sentence you. I have had the benefit of a presentence investigation and copies of this have been provided to your attorney, and I presume he has gone over that with you, is that correct?

The Defendant: *Yes, sir.*

The Court: Is there anything in there that you question, Mr. Meine?

The Defendant: *No, Your Honor. I think my attorney has explained everything pretty well.*

The Court: Is there anything in there that is factually inaccurate or something that you would like to add to the report?

The Defendant: *No, Your Honor.*

The Court: I also have the benefit of a psychological examination, and I believe copies were provided to you, Mr. Schade.

Mr. Schade: Yes, Your honor, that is true.

The Court: By virtue of this plea, Mr. Meine, you stand convicted of this offense, and it is now my obligation to pass sentence upon you. Before I do, is there any recommendation that the State has?

Mr. Tuttle: Your Honor, the State has no recommendation.

The Court: Would you state your name, please?

Mr. Tuttle: My name is Clark Tuttle and I'm the Assistant County Attorney for Brown County.

The Court: There was a plea bargain here, are you aware of that?

Mr. Tuttle: I'm aware of that.

The Court: Do you have anything you want to say on behalf of the Defendant, Mr. Schade?

Mr. Schade: Yes, Your Honor, I would. I would like to ask the Court not to impose any jail time to Mr. Meine. I would like to think that in the sentencing process we are concerned about primarily punishment and rehabilitation, and I can assure the Court that Mr. Meine has been punished up to this point, and I am sure he will be continued to be punished simply because of the publicity which has been attended to this trial.

The Court: Mr. Meine, do you have anything you want to say?

The Defendant: *No, Your Honor. I think my attorney stated it very simply.*

The Court: You don't want to add anything at all?

The Defendant: *Nothing, sir.*

The Court: Well, I presume it's something you would like to erase from your life, but you can't do it.

The Defendant: *Yes, Your Honor.*

The Court: As I indicated, I must impose a sentence for this and as punishment for this crime for which you stand convicted, you are sentenced to the Commissioner of Corrections for a period of 5 years. The execution of this sentence is stayed, and you are going to be placed on probation for that period of time, for 5 years upon some conditions which are attached to this.

The Court: I'm going to order that you pay a fine of $2,000.00 to the Clerk of Court of Brown County under such terms and installments as your probation agent can arrange with you. I understand you would not be able to pay that fine at the present time. Now, the reason why I don't put you in jail, Mr. Meine, and why I gave you the sentence that I did is because of your age and the emotional crisis that you appear to be in. I think you need the support of your family, and I would suggest also that you get some spiritual help. Your health is such that incarceration might harm you physically and mentally. I don't see that there is any likelihood or any great likelihood of your being involved in criminal conduct again.

That's all, Mr. Meine.

After the sentencing, as I look back on all the legal proceedings, I wasn't sure if justice was served. When one thinks of the magnitude of the crime Fred Meine, Jr. had committed, which was probably the largest theft of clothing in Minnesota history, I questioned whether the sentence matched the crime to which he pled guilty. His sentence of a $2,000 fine, five years probation, and some community service seemed inadequate.

At the time, I was very angry, but it was time to move on, and I realized bitterness is not a good thing for anyone, especially someone in the sales business. I would focus on working hard and rebuilding my business. I would not quit or let this ruin my career; I would persevere, and, most of all, I would learn from the experience.

Chapter 28
Life Goes On

During the hearings, I listened to Meine as he testified about his master plan to remove our inventory a few pieces at a time. Listening to Fred tell of his shopping trips to my store was very disturbing. Most bothersome was that he went into my store on Sunday morning, when the downtown was serene.

Perhaps Fred knew that we were members of the First United Methodist Church, and Sundays found us teaching school and attending worship services. This would give him the perfect two-hour timeframe to steal my merchandise. I found it quite paradoxical that these were his favorite "picking hours."

Everyone who came into the store wanted to talk about the Meine incident, and wanted me to tell the story in detail. I've heard so many versions that are not even close to the real story; each time I politely corrected the misstatements and retold it correctly.

People have frequently referred to the story or asked me to tell it to their family or friends. This is one of the reasons for my writing this book. Many times I've thought back about those days and I sometimes wonder what my life would have been like if I hadn't been robbed all those years? Would my outlook and perspective be what it is today and would I be as focused? Would I have the same appreciation for all the good things in life? Good questions, I guess.

The one question that I need to address has been asked over and over: How in the world, with the enormous amount of merchandise Fred Meine Jr.stole from you, could you not have realized what was happening?

It's hard to explain but I will try. Back in those days our business was growing by leaps and bounds. We were adding new lines of clothing, attending markets, and expanding our store size. I was young, trusting, and maybe a little naive. My young family kept me busy, as did dealing with my beloved father's illness that would eventually end his life. Ron O'Brien asked for my help in doing some coaching and motivational speaking at other Leuthold stores, taking even more of my time. At my store, I was spending almost every hour on the sales floor to keep our business above water, to pay the bills.

Reading my story you now know my desperation and despair in knowing we had a serious problem that we couldn't find the answer to. Hindsight is 20/20, and now it seems so obvious as to where and how the clothing was disappearing. In addition, when you are doing a fairly large volume of business, it's hard to notice when one or two items are missing from the racks.

Over time, I believe, as Fred became bolder, he took more and more inventory through his secret door. Did Fred think that by increasing the amount of merchandise he was stealing, he could put us out of business—and then at that point, it might go undetected?

It's also kind of a forest-for-the-trees situation that one can only understand if you were dealing with it 24/7. I have pondered this question to the point of over thinking it. Honestly, I really can't totally understand it myself—and have moved on, considering it as an experience that made me a stronger person.

It's my hope that my writing this book will bring final closure to these events, and allow me to reflect on what happened as a positive life-learning lesson of perseverance.

After a while, the talk of Fred Meine's sentencing began to die down. We were in the final stages of completing the remodeling of his former store as an addition to our existing store. The business was on the comeback, doing very well again, thus helping to stabilize our finances.

I thought about the promise I made to Konnie that we would leave New Ulm and start our lives all over somewhere else. After many conversations, we both agreed that New Ulm was our home, and we would not leave. Since we were "the victims," we really had no reason to leave our business, our home and our friends—becoming twice victimized! New Ulm is where we came to live and work; we would not let Fred Meine Jr. spoil our dream. After all, we had so much love, support, and help during the whole event, how could we leave all our friends and customers behind. The sun would rise on many new and wonderful days in New Ulm. It still does.

Our lives got pretty much back to normal after the publicity began to fade. In the process of rebuilding our business, we added a young men's department. The U.S. Male Shop was up and running in the former Meine space, and our younger customers loved it. Mitch More and Duane Lieghty were my two new employees who turned out to be super great salesmen, helping our business grow during a difficult time. Mitch now has a sporting goods business where he and Duane still work together.

Some of our store success was possible because of our great part time employees; many of these young men and women were high school and college students. They remain friends and it's so great to see the fine citizens and business people they have become.

Our store really was a family operation in every aspect. Through the years, and after our children were in school, my wife worked at the store. She eventually became our secretary and did the books after my sister, Mary, became ill with cancer and was unable to continue working. Our daughters, Amy and Sarah, both worked part-time in selling and displaying our fashions while in high school. Our sons, Chris and Eric, worked at the store during junior and senior high school days. After college, they worked full-time in the business.

Some people have asked, "Who was the most interesting employee we ever had?" My response: Mark Nichols, who moved from Colorado. Mark, who worked part time in our western wear department, is one of those people that you just never forget.

He was, and is to this day, 100 % cowboy—the real deal. For most of his life, Mark made his living ranching and training horses. If one would draw a picture of what a cowboy looks like, it would be the image of my friend, Mark Nichols, one of the most charismatic individuals I've ever met. He could charm the socks off you, and then turn around and sell them back to you.

When Mark and his wife Anne, and their two children moved to Minnesota, they purchased a farm site near Don Kassuelke's

Cowboy and roping partner Mark Nichols

place, east of New Ulm, where I boarded my horses. I was interested in team roping, and had been practicing at LeDale Johnson's place near LaSalle, Minnesota. Mark and I began to rope together, and as we got better and started to win, we competed in area rodeos. He is a great storyteller and prankster. Most everyone he meets becomes a friend. He is sincere, a great listener and would literally give you the shirt off his back, if you were in need.

Mark left New Ulm when he was hired as ranch manager for world-famous designer Ralph Lauren and his wife, Ricky, at their RR ranch in southwest Colorado. Mark and Ralph became friends while Mark managed their ranch. Mark has been photographed for numerous commercials and has been featured in articles in the New York Times and Outdoor Life Magazine about ranching and the west. I'm lucky to have such a great friend, and to have had the opportunity to ride the trails with such a great horseman and cowboy. Our Jensen Clothing customers and friends still ask about Mark to this day.

Steve Jacobson had gone on to manage his own Leuthold Store in Albert Lea, Minnesota, and later moved to Hibbing, where he and his wife, Gay (the pickle maker), still own and operate their men's and women's clothing store.

My story just wouldn't be complete without mentioning two of the finest men I ever worked with. One is Bill Hertling and the other Dan Carroll.

Bill Hertling, Dan Carroll and me

Bill Hertling came to my attention through Chico and Sandy Jensen, good friends of ours from Redwood Falls, Minnesota. Chico and Sandy knew Bill, and told us they thought he would do a great job for us. They were right!

Dan Carroll had worked at a men's clothing store in Mankato. With our store newly remodeled and expanded, and with my two new employees, we experienced fantastic growth in our sales.

Bill would become my assistant manager, a fantastic salesman and a great friend. Bill, an impeccable dresser, never had a wrinkle or trouser crease out of place. Soft-spoken, intelligent and well liked by our customers, he went about his business in a quiet way, but at the end of the day, was always one of the tops in sales. Bill and his wife, Paula, now own their men's and women's clothing store in Albert Lea.

Dan Carroll is pound for pound the most dynamic and talented salesman

I've ever known. He is also the hardest-working employee I've ever had. Dan is a handsome guy who looks terrific in a suit, as if he was posing for an advertisement in Gentlemen's Quarterly magazine. Dan had a great following in the Mankato area, and many of his customers followed him to my store. After a very successful career with us, Dan started his own business of installing carpet and tile. He is, of course, a terrific success and lives in New Ulm with his wife, Julie.

The Leuthold Company began to experience some business problems back in 1992. I was elected to take over as President, replacing Ron O'Brien. After many months of deliberation, it was decided that in the best interest of our stakeholders, that we dissolve the Leuthold Company and sell the stores to the managing partners, if they were interested. The stores were appraised and purchased by the managers, and the revenues were distributed to the shareholders.

After we purchased the Leuthold Company interest in our store, it became Jensen Clothing, Inc. In 1996, we moved our store from our long-time location on Minnesota Street to the Marktplatz Mall in the downtown area of New Ulm. We were there until 2001. The severe lack of traffic at the Mall was disappointing, and surprising to me. It was, in my

Our store in the Marktplatz Mall

opinion, an attractive mall, with good location and parking underneath. Our new space was the former Brett's Department Store. It was a beautiful store, and I thought it was one of the best-looking men's clothing stores anywhere. Our business was still strong since we were a destination-type store with a well-established base of clients.

Eric, me and Chris ready to sell suits

When Dan and Bill left to begin their new businesses, my sons, Chris and Eric, along with Konnie and I, took our store to new heights of business success. It was a thrill to work side by side with my family to reach our common goals. My sons' abilities and skills in sales, customer service and general business were the catalyst in achieving our greatest retailing years.

An interesting question posed by some people has been: What was the most interesting sale you ever made during your clothing career? Here's the story, and the answer: The phone rang at the store one day, and the caller told me he had seen an article in the Mankato Free Press about the roping club we had going at the Johnson farm near LaSalle, Minnesota. The caller asked if he could come out and watch us rope; of course I said that would be great. A few days later, he came by to observe us roping. We greeted each other, and I asked him where he was from. He told me he was working in Mankato, but lived in Oxford, Mississippi. I was quite surprised when he told me he played for the Minnesota Vikings.

Steve Freeman came to the Vikings after playing several seasons for the Buffalo Bills. Raised on a ranch in Texas, he was a good cowboy and roper. He came to our place in New Ulm and on occasion, during the time he was at training camp in Mankato, saddled up and rode our horses with me. Steve and his wife, Bo, and Konnie and I have exchanged visits and kept in touch. Steve introduced us to many of the other players, and we had the thrill of sitting with the players' families at a game against the Chicago Bears. That season, Minnesota Viking's quarterback Wade Wilson, made the Pro Bowl, and decided to buy the offensive linemen ostrich-skin cowboy boots as a thank you. He called us at the store and asked me to come to the training facility and measure up the guys. It was a big sale, and probably the most unique in my career. A side note: Paul Wyczawski who is the son of my former competitor, Red Wyczawski, was coaching baseball at the University of Mississippi, and had one of Steve and Bo's sons as a player. Paul got a kick out of learning that Konnie and I were friends of the Freemans.

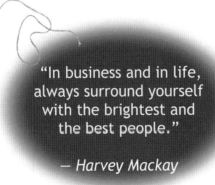

"In business and in life, always surround yourself with the brightest and the best people."

— *Harvey Mackay*

Chapter 29
The End of an Era

After thirty-six years of retailing in downtown New Ulm, we decided to sell our store. There were many reasons for our decision; among them were my concerns about the state of retailing in general, and the casual movement in the men's apparel industry. In 2001, after the sale of our store to another clothier didn't materialize, we had a store-closing sale and liquidated our inventory, ending the final chapter of Leuthold Jensen Clothing in New Ulm.

I'm so proud of our many years of retailing, and what we were able to accomplish. Our customers were extremely loyal and special to us. These days, we enjoy seeing them and catching up on their activities and families. We will always be grateful to all of our employees, customers, friends and business associates.

After the closing, our sons continued in successful business careers. Chris has his own financial investment business in North Mankato. Chris and Jayne have a daughter (our only granddaughter) and a son. Eric is in the insurance business in New Ulm; he and his wife, Bobbi, have two boys. I am so proud of the fine businessmen that Chris and Eric have become. Konnie is working part time for our son, Chris (the tables have turned—he's now her boss). Our daughter, Amy, is married to Rick Domeier (QVC host), they have two sons and live in Pennsylvania. Our youngest daughter, Sarah, has a successful career in human resource management. Married to Andy Weidman, they live in New Ulm and have three boys.

After a short period of semi-retirement, I realized I had to do something to stay busy and connected to people and business. I've had several fun and rewarding opportunities including: advertising consultant for Kohls Weelborg Chevrolet; working with the Johnson family as the Marketing Director at the I90 Expo Center Equine facility in Sherburn, Minnesota; and a second round of men's clothing sales at J. Longs in Mankato, Minnesota. Of course, I've spent the last few months finishing this book.

Today, I'm pursuing opportunities as a speaker on the topics of excellence in sales and customer service, presenting my

Me, Konnie, Eric and Rosie, our long-time tailor

motivational message to businesses and organizations. My talk includes stories from my business career, and my insights into helping re-ignite your passion for success in life and in business.

The people from New Ulm and the surrounding area have been so supportive and wonderful; we will always treasure and appreciate our friends, customers and employees. As I sit here, completing this writing journey, your names, faces and suit sizes flash through my mind! I just wish I could mention each and everyone, but I'm not able and I wouldn't want to overlook anyone.

Thanks for the memories!

"Making friends for life, our world and our situations are constantly changing. One thing that always stays the same is friendships that last forever."

Epilogue

Fred's sister, Hazel, retired from her position as Executive Secretary of the New Ulm Chamber of Commerce in March of 1979. Her retirement ended a long and distinguished Chamber career. Hazel has since passed away. Hazel and I had many conversations about what had happened as a result of Fred's confessed crime. While she was deeply hurt by what transpired, we remained friends and held no hard feelings.

Fred Meine passed away at the age of 80 at the Sleepy Eye Care Center in Sleepy Eye, Minnesota on Thursday, June 22, 2000.

After deciding to write my story, and after doing much research and many interviews with people who were involved in the ordeal in one way or another, I am convinced there is more to this story. I always wondered if Fred may have had an accomplice. This makes sense partly due to Fred's age, girth and physical condition at the time of the crime. If this is true, I will always wonder who it might have been. Perhaps, someday, I will know the truth, and could add another chapter to this story.

Moving on with my life, I forgave Fred Meine, Jr. for the crime he committed against us in the 1970s. However, I cannot forget it. To this day, it haunts me. I went to the location of the former Meine Store recently to take some photos for this story. I wanted to take pictures of the steps that led to the basement of his store. When I opened the door to his basement, I noticed a peculiar odor that I remembered from some 38 years ago. Fred's basement had an unusual smell that brought back a flood of memories.

Those difficult years have made me a stronger person. The life lessons I've learned:

• If someone knocks you down, you must get back up and fight, over and over again.

• To never fear change or challenges, but welcome them as

great opportunities.
• To appreciate and cherish relationships that last forever.
• Staying focused on success will fuel your passion to achieve your goals
• In sales, to be successful one must concentrate on great customer service with every customer. If this becomes your business culture, the sales and success will follow without question. The customer is the reason we have a job—and the reason we get a paycheck. They are the most important part of any business and should never be taken for granted. Without the customer, there is no business.

Every morning I begin my day by being thankful for what I have, and focusing on a great day. I look forward to new opportunities and experiences and friendships. My advice, is simple: Smile, be happy, dream big dreams and never give up. Be appreciative of what you have and be willing to share it with others. Communicate your appreciation to those who are special to you, and most of all, never lose your sense of humor; it is the wine of life.

Life is wonderful; don't waste a day of it!

Jim Jensen

"Success is like anything worthwhile. It has a price. You have to pay the price to win and you have to pay the price to get to the point where success is possible. Most importantly you must pay the price to stay there."

— *Vince Lombardi*

About the Author

Jim Jensen

Jim Jensen came to New Ulm, Minnesota in 1966 and was employed as a salesman for Leuthold Neubauer clothing. He enjoyed 35 years working in retail on Minnesota Street as the owner of Leuthold Jensen Clothing. Growing up on a farm near his hometown of Morgan, Minnesota, Jim fell in love with the outdoors and especially horses. This would become a lifelong hobby.

Jim and his wife, Konnie, reside in New Ulm. They have four children and nine grandchildren. Jim's business involvement includes his position as board chair of New Ulm Telecom, Inc., director for Alliance Bank, director for the Oak Hills Foundation Board, past president of the New Ulm Chamber of Commerce, past president of the New Ulm Retail Association and past director for Riverbend Center for Entrepreneurial Facilitation (a business development organization). Jim is a member of the First United Methodist Church in New Ulm and is active in numerous community organizations.

Jim is available as an inspirational speaker, specializing in topics he's passionate about—providing great customer service and excellence in sales skills.